# Customer
# Relationships

## Roger Cartwright

Fast-track route understanding the relationship between
organizations and the customer chain that contains both internal
and external customers

Covers key topics such as loyalty and customer retention. Also
explores how to move beyond customer satisfaction to customer
delight

Case studies of Amazon.com, Kalmbach Publishing (US), Boeing
(US), Saga (UK), Chowking Food Corporation (the Philippines)

Includes a comprehensive resources guide, key concepts and
thinkers, a 10-step action plan, and a section of FAQs

SALES

12.09

Copyright © Capstone Publishing, 2003

The right of Roger Cartwright to be identified as the author of this book has been asserted in accordance with the Copyright, Designs and Patents Act 1988

First Published 2003 by
Capstone Publishing Limited (a Wiley company)
8 Newtec Place
Magdalen Road
Oxford OX4 1RE
United Kingdom
http://www.capstoneideas.com

CIP catalogue records for this book are available from the British Library and the US Library of Congress

ISBN 1-84112-452-4

Wiley also publishes its books in a variety of electronic formats. Some content that appears in print may not be available in electronic books.

Websites often change their contents and addresses; details of sites listed in this book were accurate at the time of writing, but may change.

# Contents

# Introduction to ExpressExec

ExpressExec is a completely up-to-date resource of current business practice, accessible in a number of ways – anytime, anyplace, anywhere. ExpressExec combines best practice cases, key ideas, action points, glossaries, further reading, and resources.

Each module contains 10 individual titles that cover all the key aspects of global business practice. Written by leading experts in their field, the knowledge imparted provides executives with the tools and skills to increase their personal and business effectiveness, benefiting both employee and employer.

ExpressExec is available in a number of formats:

» **Print** – 120 titles available through retailers or printed on demand using any combination of the 1200 chapters available.
» **E-Books** – e-books can be individually downloaded from Express-Exec.com or online retailers onto PCs, handheld computers, and e-readers.
» **Online** – http://www.expressexec.wiley.com/ provides fully searchable access to the complete ExpressExec resource via the Internet – a cost-effective online tool to increase business expertise across a whole organization.

» **ExpressExec Performance Support Solution (EEPSS)** – a software solution that integrates ExpressExec content with interactive tools to provide organizations with a complete internal management development solution.
» **ExpressExec Rights and Syndication** – ExpressExec content can be licensed for translation or display within intranets or on Internet sites.

To find out more visit www.ExpressExec.com or contact elound@wiley-capstone.co.uk.

# Introduction to Customer Relationships

This chapter considers the following.

» The meaning of "the customer is always right."
» The global nature of business.
» The removal of monopoly status from many organizations.

"The customer is always right" has become almost a mantra for modern business. Like many well-known sayings its origin is not completely straightforward. It has been attributed to Lord Sainsbury in the UK but also to a Philadelphia department store owner, John Wannamaker, who is reputed to have first used the phrase as early as the 1860s.

Experience shows us that the customer is not always right. There are times when the customer is actually wrong, and times when he or she is not only wrong but also rude. Nevertheless the customer is the only person other than share and stockholders who brings money into an organization. No customers equals no income, which eventually equates to no organization!

The modern marketplace is increasingly becoming global. Geographic barriers no longer limit customers and potential customers. Goods can be acquired from across the globe at the keystroke of a computer connected to the Internet. The impact of the Internet on customer relationships is discussed in detail in Chapter 4. Suffice it to say it is making a massive impact.

The 1990s saw the breaking up of many monopoly situations across the world. As competition increases so also does the bargaining power of the customer. There are increasingly fewer and fewer organizations that can hold their customers hostage (a concept that is explored in both Chapters 3 and 6). Once customers discover that they have bargaining power they increasingly demand greater quality and value for money. The concept of the customer at the center of an organization's activities is now at the core of the philosophy of more and more commercial organizations.

This material forms part of the sales material for ExpressExec, but it is not just in traditional commercial selling situations that the power of the customer has grown. The years since 1980 have seen many countries deregulating and privatizing industries that had been in monopoly situations, often run entirely by the state itself.

Organizations such as the state-run British Telecom and British Airways were privatized under the Conservative government that held office from 1979 until 1997 and then had to compete within a global marketplace. For example, prior to its privatization by Margaret Thatcher's government in the 1980s, the UK telephone system was a monopoly operated by the Post Office. The monopoly was such that the Post Office not only provided the actual telephone service but also the telephone sets for the users. There was no alternative to a Post Office telephone set attached to a Post Office telephone line.

Telephone users in the UK are no longer limited in such a way for the supply of equipment or for their telephone line – they have a choice, a choice that has become even greater with the development of mobile cellular telephones. Once customers have a choice, keeping them loyal depends on delivering a service that satisfies and indeed delights them. Customer relations in a monopoly situation may become mere platitudes; in a competitive marketplace strong relationships with the customer may be the key to commercial survival.

Good customer relationships are no longer desirable – they are essential. One of the golden rules for customer service developed by the present author and his colleague, George Green, in the 1996 text *In Charge of Customer Satisfaction* was: "Look after your customers because if you don't somebody else will."

Commercial history is full of organizations that did not take heed of similar advice.

# What is Meant by Customer Relations?

This chapter considers the following concepts relating to customer relations.

» Who is the customer?
» The nature of exchange.
» The customer chain.
» Added value.
» Internal and external customers.
» Needs and wants.
» Grudge purchases.
» Definition of customer relations.
» Customer driven and product led.
» Repeat business.
» Lifetime value.
» Definition of products and services.

Before beginning to consider how organizations relate to their customers it is necessary to consider who the customer actually is.

## WHO IS THE CUSTOMER?

In legal terms, in the vast majority of the jurisdictions in the world, the answer to the above question is relatively simple. The customer is the person, persons or organization that contracts with another for the supply of goods or services.

Person A wishes to buy a hotdog at a ball game. Person A approaches a vendor – B – and exchanges money for a hotdog. A simple transaction where there is no doubt who the customer is; or is there?

If person A has bought the hotdog for child C then the views and opinions of C cannot be ignored. Person A might not have bought anything from the vendor if he or she had not been asked to do so by C. The legal customer in this scenario is purely an intermediary between vendor B and C, the end user of the product. In most jurisdictions children are not allowed to enter into legally binding contracts, so that any problems that occur with the transaction have to be dealt with by an adult representing the child.

Customers are those for whom the individual or organization satisfies a need. The need may be for food or drink, or a computer, or medical services. Organization A might supply steel to organization B – an organization that builds ships. Organization B needs steel because without it the organization cannot satisfy its customers. Most transactions involve a chain of customers as shown in Fig. 2.1.

Supplier A → B → C → D, etc. → Purchaser → End user

**Fig. 2.1** The customer chain.

Organization/supplier B is a customer of A; C is a customer of B etc. It is important to realize that the purchaser and the end user may not be one and the same but that there is likely to be considerable feedback between them. In the customer chain an organization has not only to satisfy its immediate customer but also that customer's customer. Each step along the customer chain adds value to the product or service.

## ADDED VALUE

The concept of adding value can be demonstrated by considering a simplified production line. As each component is added to a product in the course of its assembly the value of the product goes up by the value of the component plus the value to the customer of having the component added. It is possible to put together an automobile, a private aircraft, a boat and even a house from a kit of parts at a cost that is usually much less than buying the ready made product.

Why don't more people take this approach and save themselves money? The answer is simple: most people do not have either the skills or, more importantly, the time to do so. A component of the cost of any product/service must reflect the perceived value that the customer places on the skills of those producing the product/service and the time saved by the customer in purchasing it rather than doing it his or her self. Not only *could* we build our own cars, but we could make our clothes, erect our own homes and even carry out our own legal tasks. For most people however it is a lack of time to both acquire the skills and carry out the task that stops them. Time is an opportunity cost and the value of the time is greater than the price charged for the skills and time of those delivering the product/service.

Each step in the process of delivering a product/service contains a skill/time cost and a monetary amount of added value that the customer is prepared to pay. This is known as a value chain with the costs of the product building up at each step together with a contribution to the added value. The costs of a process consist of a series of factors.

Cost of raw materials + Cost of labor + Contribution to the overheads

of the organization + Extra costs(marketing, distribution etc.)

Adding these costs together gives the cost to the organization. The price the customer is prepared to pay should be the total costs above plus the opportunity cost to the customer of not making the product his or herself. That opportunity cost represents profit to the organization.

A restaurant is a good example of the above. The price of the meal is usually far greater than the total cost of the ingredients and the restaurateur's other costs (wages, premises etc.). People often say, "I could cook that myself for far less." True but have they the time?

## INTERNAL AND EXTERNAL CUSTOMERS

Thus there are two main categories of customers: internal and external.

It is the external customer who provides profit whilst each internal customer adds value. Each person or process along the value chain is a customer of the preceding person or process.

The automobile assembly worker who fits the wheels to an axle is an internal customer of the worker who assembles the axle. The axle assembler is an internal supplier. He or she relies on their supplier to give them an axle they can attach a wheel to. The better the internal customer relationships are, the more likely it is that the external customer will be well treated.

## DEFINITION

Taking all of the above into consideration a customer can be defined as:

» Somebody for whom you satisfy a need.

In psychological terms needs are very basic. Humans, like all other animals, have a need for food, water, shelter etc. Wants are enhanced needs. I need food, I want a steak and French fries; I need liquid, I want a gin and tonic; I need shelter, I want a condominium in Florida.

Good customer relations goes beyond satisfying the customer's needs as it also *delights the customer in terms of wants*.

## GRUDGE PURCHASES

Most of the products and services that customers acquire they not only need (i.e. they are necessary) but they also want. Grudge purchases however include those things that people need but do not want or do not want to pay for. A person may need to visit the dentist but it is unlikely that they will want to be in the situation where such a visit is necessary. We need funeral directors, prisons, law enforcement etc. But most people, whilst recognizing the need, would rather not have to pay for them. Governments that say they are going to put up taxes as part of a manifesto commitment to increase public spending often find that whilst every user of such services agrees with increasing funding, that same person speaking as a tax payer wants lower taxes. In polling booths it is often the taxpayer part of people that decides where the vote is going.

## CUSTOMER RELATIONS

Customer relations is more than just providing excellent service and care at the point of a transaction. Relationships, by the very meaning of the word, have a temporal span; they have a beginning, a middle and unfortunately an end over a span of time. Relationships also need effort in establishing them and there are vital maintenance functions. Relationship is a neutral word: relationships can be either good or bad, we can love or hate but these extremes are still just relationships. It is a good relationship that every organization should seek with its customers not just a relationship per se. Equally each internal supplier needs a good relationship with his or her internal customers.

### Customer driven versus product led

There are two extremes to a relationship with the customer and indeed to marketing as a whole. An organization that adopts a *product led approach*, develops products and systems that are suited to the organization and then tries to sell them. Henry Ford expressed this approach well in the 1920s when he offered customers a Model T Ford in "any color as long as it's black." Such an approach can work in a situation where there is no competition and demand exceeds supply.

A *customer driven approach* is one that considers the needs of the customer first and then seeks to satisfy those needs. The movement from product led to customer driven is considered in more detail in Chapter 3.

Many organizations claim that they put the customer at the center of their operations but experience shows that this is sometimes a false belief. The organizations in Chapter 7 are ones that do have the customer very clearly at the center of their operations and indeed at the center of their value system.

## REPEAT BUSINESS

Good customer relationships greatly increase the potential for repeat business – one of the most important performance indicators for those involved with sales. Making an initial sale should not be the only indicator of success; indeed it is making the next sale to the same customer that is the acid test of customer satisfaction.

High pressure selling where gaining a sale is all-important may be counter-productive if the customer has felt pressurized into making the purchase – he or she may be unwilling to deal with the organization again and may even tell colleagues and friends about the pressure, alienating them from the selling organization.

## LIFETIME VALUE

A sales representative in an automobile dealer's sells a new vehicle costing $16,000 to a customer–what is the potential value of that sale?

It is potentially far more than $16,000. There is the value of spare parts and servicing to be added but there is also the value of potential future sales. Over a lifetime a customer may spend upwards of $200,000 on automobiles starting with pre-owned ones in his or her youth and the latest model when well into a career. A large number of people change their vehicle at regular intervals. So the $16,000 sale may represent potential future sales of up to $200,000 depending where the customer is in his or her motoring career.

Each step along the customer chain adds value to the product or service depending where the individual is in his or her owner-ship continuum. The salesperson should not be thinking of just the immediate gain but of all the future potential business represented in that customer if he or she can be kept loyal to the product and the dealership.

## KEY LEARNING POINTS

### The customer is somebody for whom you satisfy a need

» Effective customer relations not only satisfies needs but also delights in respect of customer wants.

» There is often a customer chain in which each customer is satisfied by the preceding one and then satisfies the next customer in the chain.

» Value is added along the customer chain.

» Internal customers may be just as important as external ones.

» Organizations operate along a continuum from product led to customer driven.

» Grudge purchases are those purchases that a customer needs but does not want.

» Customers should not be considered in terms of a single transaction but for their lifetime value through repeat business.

# The Evolution
# of Customer Relations

This chapter examines the evolution of customer relations and shows the following.

» The development of mass production brought about by the industrial revolution distanced many manufacturers and suppliers from their customers.
» The distancing of suppliers/manufacturers from their customers led to a growth in retail operations.
» There has been a change in organizational orientation from product orientation to a selling, marketing and lately a customer orientation.
» Customers are becoming more sophisticated.
» Supplementary products may be just as important as the core product in the buying decision.
» Repeat business is just as important a performance criterion as the initial sale.

There have been relationships between suppliers and customers since humankind began trading. There are only two means for an individual, organization or country to acquire something that is perceived as a need. The first method is to use some form of force–theft war etc.–and the other is to enter into an exchange.

The exchange method is what is known as trade. Party A has something that party B wants. Provided that party B is in possession of something that party A perceives to be of equivalent value to the good that B wants from A trade can take place (a good – this should be a singular noun as it is an economic term for any item used in trade).

Rather than bartering a good for a good (although this is a method often used by governments who may pay for weapons with oil etc.) most transactions use a common denominator that has become known as money.

For there to be a fruitful relationship between A and B both need to gain from the transaction – it needs to be a win/win situation. If A (the seller) wins by obtaining more than expected then B loses and may not wish to trade with A again. If A loses because B strikes too hard a bargain then A may not wish to have B as a customer. If both lose then there is no point in the relationship. It may be to A's advantage to lose a little, perhaps by offering a loss leader – something that is sold at below its value to elicit further business.

It is not in a customer's long-term interest to obtain bargain after bargain. If the supplier is not making enough money out of the transactions sooner or later the price must rise or the supplier goes out of business. As it is competition that keeps prices down then the loss of a supplier means fewer choices and thus the probability of higher prices for the customer.

The well-known and respected US marketing authority Michael Porter has written about the relative bargaining powers of suppliers and customers. The balance between the two has not been constant but has been shifting in favor of the customer since the middle 1800s. During the intervening years the orientation adopted by business has shifted from a product orientation (product led) to that of a customer orientation (customer driven).

Prior to industrialization the relationships between supplier and customer tended to be more personal. To take an item of furniture as an example, today the vast majority of people will purchase furniture from a retailer rather than from the actual maker. Before furniture could be mass-produced pieces were made as commissions either by a local handyman or if the customer was wealthy by a renowned maker. A similar situation existed in the clothing market–people either made their own or went in person to a seamstress or tailor. Most clothing today is purchased from a shop and the maker and customer seldom meet save for the most expensive, bespoke garments.

## MASS PRODUCTION

The industrial revolution brought into being the concept of mass production. Whilst mass-production is often thought of as a twentieth century innovation it actually began in the nineteenth century. The introduction of the mechanical loom enabled cloth to be woven in large quantities, while the development of the steam press provided a means of pressing out identical metal components also in large quantities.

Mass production increased the distance between the manufacturer and the customer. At the same time the development of railways and steam ships increased the distance over which ordinary goods could be transported cheaply. Not only was there a growth in manufacturing but a parallel growth in retail operations to link manufacturers and customers.

## PRODUCT ORIENTATION

From the beginning of the industrial revolution in the early nineteenth century right through to the end of World War I, many organizations adopted a product orientation. This is a philosophy that encompasses a belief that if products are of high enough quality and at a reasonable price, then sufficient customers will buy them. Market research, as we know it today, was not seen as being necessary. It was a time of a plethora of new products with patents being filed at an ever-increasing rate. Many products failed to be successful but enough were and thus ensured the survival of many organizations.

It is difficult to see how a modern consumer would accept Henry Ford's "you can have any color so long as it is black" statement. Ford's

Model T looks antiquated to modern eyes but it was state of the art when it came out in the early part of the twentieth century. Demand for personal transport in the USA was so great that there was no need to seek the views of the customer. Ford could sell every Model T they could manufacture. The balance of power between the supplier and the customer was very much to the former's benefit.

Unfortunately too many motorcar manufacturers persisted in ignoring the views of an increasingly sophisticated customer base and persisted in manufacturing a product that failed to meet modern trends. The success of the Japanese motor industry was in a large part due to the way it listened to customers and provided what they wanted. In recent years both US and European automobile manufacturers have changed their attitudes considerably and are now seen as much more customer centered.

## SELLING ORIENTATION

A product orientation can succeed as long as demand is greater than supply. As demand and supply converge, organizations need to be more active in actually selling the product. This is especially true as competition grows. A selling orientation recognizes that consumers may be reluctant to buy and need to be "sold" the product or service. The years from the 1920s through to the 1950s were very much selling oriented. It was in this period that selling techniques became a legitimate area of study. Many organizations still have a selling orientation but others have moved on to a marketing/customer orientation as described below. Prior to this period advertisements tended to adopt a basic 'factual' approach – this is what it is, this is what it does and this is what it costs. Even if the claims made were exaggerated the advertising techniques were very straightforward.

The selling orientation shifts the balance between the product and the customer towards the latter.

## MARKETING ORIENTATION

A key role of marketing is to ease the sales process. The more that an organization knows about its customers and their requirements, the less effort will be needed in the sale's process. If effort is put into understanding the customer, that customer is more likely to buy. From the 1960s onward, more and more organizations adopted a marketing orientation whereby marketing information became a major component of the design process. As more and more information about customers was acquired so the balance between product and customer became more and more biased towards the customer.

## CUSTOMER ORIENTATION

By the latter years of the twentieth century many organizations had adopted a customer orientation where the customer was an integral part of the organization's processes. A customer oriented organization involves customers at as many stages of product/service design, development and implementation as possible.

In a highly competitive environment the more the organization knows about the needs of the customer and the easier it is to reach the customer, the more it will be able to compete. When Tom Peters and Bob Waterman coined the phrase "close to the customer" they were articulating a concept that was becoming more and more apparent – organizations that do not get close to their customers run the risk of somebody else doing so.

The work of Jones and Strasser, to be reviewed in Chapter 6, showed that many loyal customers were not loyal at all – they just had no choice. Once a choice was provided the customers defected and they defected to organizations that made an attempt to get close to them.

## CHANGING ATTITUDES OF CUSTOMERS

As stated in Chapter 1, the immortal phrase, "the customer is always right" was coined in the 1860s by John Wannamaker, a Philadelphia department store owner (popular belief in the UK ascribes the remarks to John Sainsbury and perhaps there is nothing wrong with two different groups claiming ownership in this instance!).

The retail trade, dependent as it was – and remains – on good face-to-face, continuing relationships with customers, was far quicker to pick up on the importance of delivering customer satisfaction and the idea that the customer should always be treated as if he or she is right.

By the early 1900s the steamship companies taking immigrants from Europe to North America had upgraded their immigrant or "steerage" accommodation considerably. As Davie (1986) has pointed out, this was less as a result of official rules on the transportation of immigrants and more to do with a realization that there was profit to be made in attracting the immigrant trade and that those who went out steerage might, having done well in the New World (Canada and the US) make visits home using second or even first class. If they had been impressed by the steerage accommodation they might well book themselves and their families in higher-priced cabins for visits to their ancestral homes. Whilst books on the Atlantic liner trade often concentrate on the first-class passengers and the sumptuous accommodation they had available it was, in fact, the steerage passengers who provided the profits for the companies operating the ships. First-and second-class fares covered the overheads with profits coming out of the third/steerage fares.

As competition has increased, so the suppliers of goods and services have had to woo their customers. The ability to travel brought about firstly by the railways and then by the motor car and the airplane has increased the radius that a customer is able to go in order to fulfill their requirements. Town center and even city center shops have found it difficult to compete with supermarkets situated on the outskirts of town, especially when those supermarkets provide good parking facilities, petrol pumps, and in some cases buses for those without cars. Customers today are prepared to look further and further afield not just for the lowest prices but also for enhanced service and facilities. Contemporary retail developments tend to be of the large shopping mall type encompassing a number of shops, banks, restaurants etc.

Customers have become used to choice and quality. Today's customer challenges and wants to know the why and not just the how. The medical and legal professions, local and national government, newly privatized industries, and education have all been required to become more responsive to the needs of their customers.

The development of improved communication systems after World War II, in particular the telephone and the television, helped bring about a consumer revolution. It became much easier for consumers to exchange information, and the development of commercial broadcasting, firstly in the United States and then in Europe, meant that viewers were exposed to increasing amounts of advertising, making them more aware of the choices available in the marketplace.

In 1965 a young US lawyer and freelance political consultant named Ralph Nader published a book entitled *Unsafe at Any Speed* (Nader, 1965) in which he attacked the lack of concern for consumer safety amongst the US automobile industry. Ralph Nader's efforts, which many have described as a crusade, grew to encompass not only the safety of motor vehicles but also many other areas of interest to US consumers from sport to nuclear power.

Nader and his "Raiders" (as he and his seven associates were known) became feared by corporate America and as Celsi (1991) reports he became "the nation's self-appointed consumer advocate." Nader's work led to the US Congress setting up the Consumer Protection Agency in 1970. The 1960s was a time of social revolution in western society, the music of Bob Dylan et al fuelling the revolutionary fervor of a generation of teenagers and young adults. Civil rights were a huge issue in the US and Nader's consumer revolution fitted neatly into the pattern. For too long the huge corporations had been able to operate in a manner that assumed that they knew what the customer wanted. The consumers began to fight back and demanded quality and service. The signs had been there for some time. Just after World War II, Ford designers had developed what they believed would be the best automobile they had ever produced, the Ford Edsel named after Henry Ford's son. Unfortunately they never consulted with the potential customers and whilst the vehicle might have been technologically advanced, it did not meet the needs of the customer. It is ironic that the Edsel has now obtained cult status amongst the vintage vehicle and classic auto fraternity with examples being snapped up as soon as they are advertised.

In the UK, Nader's work was followed closely. Even before he became a household name on both sides of the Atlantic, the Consumer's Association had been founded in 1957 and began publication of the magazine *Which*. The magazine tested products and provided an independent guide to consumers.

In 1982, Tom Peters and Bob Waterman published *In Search of Excellence*, their study of successful US companies, and made the point that closeness to the customer and active listening to customers were key attributes for successful companies (Peters & Waterman, 1982). A similar study in the UK by Goldsmith and Clutterbuck drew remarkably similar conclusions. *The Winning Streak* (as they entitled it) demonstrated that successful UK companies were those that spent time developing customer relations (Smith & Clutterbuck, 1984).

## REPEAT BUSINESS

More and more sales success is being determined not by the number of initial sales but the amount of repeat business that a sale generates.

Selling techniques can assist in gaining an initial sale but repeat sales will only be made if the customer is satisfied with the product or service.

Once repeat sales become a performance indicator, the sales staff has a vested interest in product/service quality. The sales staff becomes a two-way conduit between the customer and those producing the product/service. One of the roles of modern sales staff is to provide the organization with customer feedback in order to improve product/service delivery.

## CORE AND SUPPLEMENTARY PRODUCTS

A further step in the evolution of customer relations has been in the importance of supplementary products. Most products are comprised of two components, a core product that is designed to meet the customer's main need requirements and a supplementary that supports the core.

Most modern automobiles are basically very similar. Any modern automobile purchased from new should be of acceptable quality and fit for the purpose for which it was intended. Many of the automobiles sold look very similar. It is in the area of the supplementary products that buying decisions are often made. Power steering (rapidly becoming a part of the core product), extra safety features, air conditioning, the sound system, satellite navigation, and the after-sales service offered are often the reasons for buying the product from one manufacturer rather than another. Customers are only too well aware that there is no use in acquiring a dream auto if the company/dealership cannot provide a quality after-sales service. It is not in the manufacturer or dealer's interest not to offer excellent after-sales service, as they will wish the customer to buy another of their autos in the future.

## THE INTERNET

The development of e-commerce since the mid-1990s has produced an extra dimension to customer relations by further breaking down barriers of distance. The implications of e-commerce for customer relations are discussed in the next chapter.

## TIMELINE

Figure 3.1 shows the evolution of customer relations.

### KEY LEARNING POINTS

» The phrase "the customer is always right" dates from the 1860s.
» The modern customer is more sophisticated than his or her predecessors.
» Organizations need to adopt a customer orientation.
» Repeat business is an important sales performance criterion.
» Products and services comprise both a core and a supplementary component.

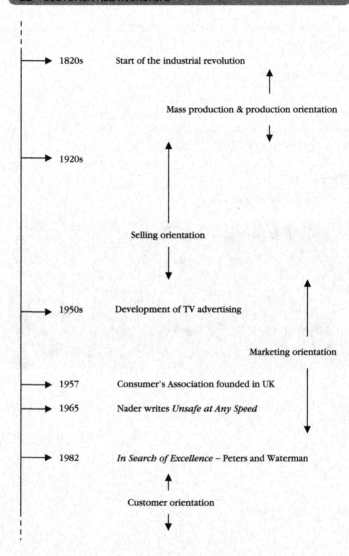

**Fig. 3.1** Evolution of customer relations timeline.

# The E-Dimension to Customer Relationships

This chapter explores the e-dimension to customer relationships and explains:

» how e-commerce has its roots in mail order;
» how companies undertaking e-commerce need a set of special attributes and skills; and
» how amazon.com has revolutionized book selling.

From a twenty-first century viewpoint, e-commerce (the term given to business transactions carried out electronically over the Internet) is a logical development from the mail order operations that began in the nineteenth century and are still in use today.

As was explained in the last chapter there have always been those who are remote from the source of the goods and services they require but want an easy method of acquiring them.

Just as mail order required the development of reliable mail services so e-commerce needs the customer to be convinced of the reliability of the transaction systems. What tends to worry potential customers the most are the dangers of credit card fraud and dishonest traders who either do not deliver what they have been paid for or deliver something of much lower quality than the customer expected.

Patricia Seybold (1998) has listed the following eight critical success factors for managing customer relationships in e-commerce operations. Many of them are just as appropriate for a small town store.

» Target the right customers.
» Own the customer's total experience.
» Streamline business processes that impact the customer.
» Provide a 360-degree view of the customer relationship.
» Let customers help themselves.
» Deliver personalized service.
» Foster community.
» Help customers do their jobs.

To achieve success she believes that there are five key steps that an organization entering e-commerce needs to take:

» make it easy for customers to do business with you;
» focus on the end customer for your products and services;
» redesign your customer-facing business processes from the end customer's point of view;
» design a comprehensive, evolving electronic business architecture; and
» foster customer loyalty.

To Seybold's factors and steps must be added the provision of secure financial procedures that protect the customer from any form of fraud.

The Internet began in the US with the linking together of a series of computers known as DARPA (Defence Agency Research Projects Administration) to form what became known in 1969 as ARPAnet, and was originally designed to protect military communications in the event of a nuclear attack – a very real fear in the political climate of the time. The system used three university hosts in California and one in Utah. Later in the 1970s the US academic community set up a purely civilian network funded by the NSF (National Science Foundation) that linked an increasing number of US and foreign universities via NSFnet. For the first time academics and researchers could communicate text via a new medium: electronic mail, rapidly contracted to e-mail.

As students who had used e-mail began to take up positions within the private sector it was not long before large commercial organizations in the US, beginning with the computer companies such as IBM and Hewlett-Packard, began to talk to each other via e-mail linking their systems to the NSFnet.

In 1993 Marc Andreessen and his group at the University of Illinois introduced the first web browser software (Mosaic), a software application for the UNIX operating system but later adapted for Apple Macintosh and Microsoft Windows®. NSFnet gradually became less relevant and the commercial world saw the birth of ISPs (Internet Service Providers) so that by the middle of the 1990s organizations in both the public and private sectors were not only using e-mail but were beginning to design and post web pages. The World Wide Web had been born. Once web use began to grow it was only natural that companies would seek to gain competitive advantage by using it to expand their customer base.

## AMAZON.COM

Globally, Amazon.com is probably one of the best-known names of the new dot.com companies that seemed to spring up (and sometimes disappear just as quickly) at the end of the 1990s and into the early years of the new century. Amazon has become successful by a careful consideration of who its customers and potential customers are and how the company can meet their needs.

The founder of amazon.com, ex-Princeton graduate Jeff Bezos is the son of a Cuban immigrant to the US. Bezos's first job (on his vacation whilst still a student) was as a programmer/analyst for his father's company, the oil giant Exxon.

Upon leaving Princeton, Bezos became involved with the computer side of the banking industry and began to see the potential of the Internet for commerce. It is now generally agreed that the birth of the World Wide Web was in 1993 (Spector, 2000). But even before that the proactive were registering their names. Amongst them were a very small number of booksellers, the first being Computer Literacy. Research that Bezos carried out for his then employer in 1994 showed that Internet usage was growing at an incredible 2300 percent per annum. Bezos decided to consider exactly which products/services would suit the Internet as a supplier-customer interface. His choices included software, clothing and books and it became apparent from his research that books, a product going back centuries, were a very good choice for the most up-to-date medium of trade.

The book trade has always been fragmentary with a large number of publishers in different countries together with retail outlets ranging from small, independent one-site operations to national and latterly international chains. Spector (2000) reports that in the US even the largest of the publishers, Random House, had less than 10 percent of the market and that the two largest retail chains, Barnes and Nobel and Borders (who also have a large UK operation), accounted for less than 25 percent of the $30 billion of adult sales in 1994.

However, as reading is a popular activity book selling is big business – in 1996 global book sales netted $82 billion. In the UK the 1990s saw a deregulation within the industry with the scrapping of the net book agreement that had fixed prices. Booksellers could now discount and the major chains did just that, three for two deals etc. on novels becoming increasingly common. In the US this trend had been led by Crown Books in the 1980s.

The major problem that traditional bookstores have always had is the need for space for selling and warehousing. Even the largest store in the US or UK could only carry a small percentage of the 1.5 million English language books in print at any one time.

Bezos realized that a virtual bookstore using the Internet could place no limit on the number of titles available to the customer. His operation could acquire stock direct from the publishers or from one of the small number of book distributors. The Internet technology would make the customer's task of searching for a title relatively simple and a check could be kept on customer preferences so that recommendations could be made, thus personalizing the service to the same level as possible when using a small independent bookstore on a regular basis. There, it is the owner who knows the customer; in the Bezos vision it is the computer.

Moving to Seattle, Bezos spent much of 1994 meeting people and learning about the book business whilst conducting an analysis of the market and the competition. In November 1994, Bezos and his associates began the amazon.com operation in a converted garage in a section of Seattle, using a database of books in print and information from the Library of Congress. (Look at the front of nearly any book in the English language that is likely to reach the US or UK markets and you will find Library of Congress and The British Library statements that the book is included in their catalogues.)

The company was launched to the public in 1995 by which time it had acquired a database of more than one million titles. An ordering system, customer identification system, distribution, and the all important credit card facilities had been established. No longer need people with access to the Internet (a growing percentage of the US population) travel to a bookstore. No matter how remote they were, they could browse the book lists online and order with confidence. The only thing they could not do was to scan the shelves and the pages of the books on them. However more and more information about content is available in the media, on the Internet and on the amazon.com site itself.

The way amazon.com (amazon.co.uk, amazon.de etc.) is set up for e-commerce the customer is presented with a virtual bookstore containing a huge number of titles and a search facility that requires only the minimum of computer skills.

From the beginning, amazon.com discounted their best sellers by 10 percent with some titles discounted by up to 30 percent. The writer of this material lives in the north of Scotland and has found over a period of using amazon.co.uk that the discount offered usually wipes out the postage costs. As the nearest conventional bookshop is 20 miles away from him with the larger shops being about 50 miles distant, a considerable time and financial saving is made by ordering on line.

Provided that the user does not delete the amazon "cookie" from his or her system the site provides a degree of a personal relationship. Upon entering the site after the first order has been placed, a personal "welcome back" message is provided. Based on previous purchasing patterns, news of the latest releases in the customer's particular areas of interest is also provided. Small booksellers have long provided such personal service based on a knowledge of the customer's interests, a service that the major retailers cannot provide. By the use of ICT (Information and Communication Technology) an on-line operation such as Amazon is able to provide a personal service that mimics that of the smaller booksellers.

Like the vast majority of the early dot.com operations Bezos lost money - $303,000 in 1995. However, even so early on in the history of the company over 2000 people per day were visiting the site and within two years this would increase to 80,000.

By 1996 Bezos had acquired sufficient venture capital to expand the amazon.com operation, the company had increased to 150 employees, and, more importantly, had produced $16 million in sales - prompting an approach from the major bookseller, Barnes and Noble, although no deal materialized. Also in that year an associates program was launched whereby the owners of other Websites could direct their visitors to amazon.com and receive a small payment if this resulted in a purchase.

In 1997, amazon.com made its IPO (initial public offering). Despite the fact that the company was still losing money, nearly $5 million in the first quarter of 1997, sales had boomed and investors considered Amazon.com worth buying and the IPO was oversubscribed. The opening price was $18 and after an initial rise and fall ended the year at $52 - not bad for a company that had only made losses.

## Global expansion

In 1998 Bezos began talks with Bertelsmann AG, the German media giant that already had a small bookselling operation, BOL. This led to nothing for amazon.com but Bertelsmann later acquired 50 percent of the Barnes and Noble online operation - competition was growing. Amazon then acquired a UK online operation and a smaller online bookshop in Germany. This gave Bezos an entry into the lucrative UK and German markets. The UK was important, as London is a large publishing center for English language books. Most of the major publishers operate parallel UK (often London) and US (New York or Cambridge MA) operations.

These moves led to the formation of amazon.co.uk in the UK and amazon.co.de in Germany. As has been stated in this material, the addition of the local country Web designators – .uk and .de – gives the customer the feeling that they are dealing with a national supplier and not a foreign interloper. A small example of this is that the customer loads their purchases onto a shopping cart on amazon.com but into a shopping basket on amazon.co.uk, where US published and supplied books are dual priced in dollars and pounds sterling.

This expansion has led to certain copyright problems. US copyright law bars the importation of copyrighted books for commercial resale (but not for private use). Bezos considered that a US citizen buying from amazon.co.uk (easily accessed from the US) was just the same as flying to London, buying the book and bringing it back to the US. This argument is still ongoing. Certainly users of amazon.co.uk have no difficulty in acquiring US books through the site, as the writer can testify. The decision to expand into the UK and Germany was sensible, as much of the British Commonwealth will happily buy from the UK and central Europeans are accustomed to doing business with German companies. With its local distribution systems, amazon.co.uk and its German counterpart have grown rapidly to become an established part of the local book-buying scene.

By 1999, Amazon as a group had expanded into CD and DVD sales through its online Zshops and in 2001 started to sell electronic items including cameras. In 1999 total sales were $2.6 billion and again in 2001 Amazon acquired the Borders online operation.

By 2001 the global expansion had included two further very important markets – France and Japan. Where next? China, India, which both have large populations and avid readers?

There is no doubt that despite the problems of the dot.com companies and the time it takes to move into profit, Bezos has provided the world with an effective means of buying an old product – the humble book is as important today as it has been throughout history for the transmission of knowledge, culture, and ideas and for providing sheer pleasure through reading.

## Browsing

In this instance browsing is used in its book buying rather than its Internet sense. One of the pleasures in buying a book is gained through browsing the stock in the bookstore before making a purchase.

This is difficult to do when using an on-line bookstore. However Amazon is increasing the ability of users to browse through the titles. By 2002 users of the main US amazon.com site were able to read sample pages of an increasing range of books and it is understood that this facility will soon be available on the amazon sites in other countries.

Amazon allows the customer to search by title, author, ISBN, publisher and keyword, making it relatively simple to track down the required titles.

A large number of the titles listed by Amazon contain both a synopsis and reviews from readers. Amazon provides an easy to use review facility for readers to make comments available for other users. Whilst one cannot actually hold the book and flick through the pages, Amazon is trying to simulate this as nearly as possible.

By not only providing details of a book following a user search but also displaying a list headed "others who bought this title also bought books by......" The site uses its analytical power to guide the user to other titles that may be of interest. As stated earlier once a purchase has been made the customer's preference list will be re-evaluated to take account of the new purchase.

## Payment

Payments on the Amazon sites are made by credit card using a secure server. The customer has the choice of completing the full order form or, if he or she feels confident about security, using a one-click facility that allows for the financial details to be completed automatically using stored credit card details. The customer has 90 minutes in which to change his or her mind before the order is confirmed.

All orders are confirmed by e-mail and a second e-mail is sent as soon as the goods are dispatched.

Customers can have items sent to another address – facilitating the sending of presents – and it is also possible to send Amazon gift vouchers that the recipient can redeem on the site.

## Delivery

With the exception of e-books, the vast majority of the products that Amazon supplies require delivery through postal and courier services. The packaging is excellent and provides good protection for the product. Presents can be gift wrapped with a personalized label making Amazon an ideal means of sending gifts.

## Handling problems

Problems that can occur with a purchase include products not being suited to a customer's needs. As he or she has had to browse in a virtual environment what seems ideal on the screen may disappoint when it arrives. No problem – the customer can return the product and his or her credit card account will be refunded. The same for non-delivery or even if the same item has been ordered twice – as this writer once did by accident!

If an item is delayed, Amazon keeps the customer informed allowing him or her to make the choice as to whether to cancel the order or keep it live.

Comparing Amazon to Seybold's eight attributes as introduced at the start of this chapter it is easy to see why the company has attracted so many customers. Amazon, like all the companies profiled in this material, has gone to considerable lengths to center the product on the customer's needs and to engage with the customer in a partnership rather than a temporary relationship.

## AMAZON.COM TIMELINE

- » **1994**: Bezos begins planning Amazon.
- » **1995**: Amazon.com launched in US.
- » **1996**:Venture capital put into Amazon.
- » **1997**: Initial Public Offering of Amazon stock.
- » **1998**: Expansion into UK and Germany.
- » **1999**: Amazon expands into CD and DVD sales.
- » **2000**: Expansion into France and Japan.
- » **2001**: Borders online operation acquired. Expansion into electronic items.

## KEY LEARNING POINTS

» As a virtual store Amazon can offer far more titles than a store that requires warehousing facilities.

» By including reviews and sample materials Amazon allows the user to browse its virtual bookshelves.

» "Cookies" and analysis of purchase patterns allow Amazon to personalize the service offered.

» Credit card payments are made using a secure server.

» There is a robust returns policy.

» There is a partnership and engagement with the customer.

# Global Implications
# for Customer Relations

This chapter considers the implications for customer relations of operating in a global marketplace. It explains:

» how organizations need to understand customer concerns regarding payments and complaints;
» how organizations can only develop a good relationship with foreign customers if they take cultural differences into account; and
» why global success is best achieved by "thinking globally but acting locally."

One of the effects of the growth of e-commerce as covered in the previous chapter has been the increase in global operations. The wider the geographic area a company can cover, the larger the potential customer base. Once a company moves out of its country of origin however, customer relationships may become more problematic for the following reasons.

» The customer may be concerned about payment methods and currency fluctuations.
» There may well be concerns about the return of faulty items and the availability of routine maintenance.
» Customers often prefer to acquire a home produced product for patriotic reasons.

## PAYMENT METHODS AND CURRENCY FLUCTUATIONS

Customers will wish to pay in their own currency whilst the supplier may well be happier with the currency of its home base. Credit card companies will adjust payments between currencies although there is always the issue of a change in the relative values of the currencies used for the transaction between placing an order and delivery and payment.

It may be possible to agree a payment currency – this is often done in the case of large company-to-company or government transactions. The US dollar is often used as a mutually acceptable currency. A majority of European Union (EU) members have adopted the Euro as their common currency.

It is to a company's customer relations advantage to use the currency of the customer.

## RETURN OF FAULTY ITEMS AND AVAILABILITY OF ROUTINE MAINTENANCE

The further away a company is from the customer, the more likely it is that the customer will be concerned about what will happen if there is a problem with the product.

As the geographic area covered by an increasing number of companies has grown so has the need for them to "think globally but act locally." Electronic manufacturers such as Samsung and Toyota, automobile manufacturers such as Ford and Volkswagen, and aircraft manufacturers (Boeing and Airbus Industrie) all sell their products to a global marketplace but they do so through offices, agents and licensees in the individual geographic markets.

The customer is able to deal with a local agent etc. who speaks the same language. As shown below there are nearly always local differences in brand names, specification, packaging etc., and in many cases these reassure the customer that although he or she has acquired a global product it is one that is customized (however slightly for his or her own market) and that there will be local support available in case of any difficulties.

## HOME PRODUCED VERSUS FOREIGN PRODUCTS

One of the reasons for "thinking globally but acting locally" is the predisposition of many customers to favor a local product over a foreign one. The more local a product can be made to seem, the easier it may be to overcome any customer resistance.

## CULTURE

Culture is considered in detail in the ExpressExec material, *Managing Diversity*. Culture can be defined as the "way we do things around here" and differs from place to place across the globe, between ethnic groups and between organizations. There is fortunately a wealth of material on managing cultural differences and the reader is advised to consult *Managing Diversity* (Chapters 5 and 6) in this series, *Riding the Waves of Culture* by Fons Trompenaars, *When Cultures Collide* by Richard D Lewis and *Managing Cultural Differences* by Philip Harris and Robert Moran (details of these texts are given in Chapter 9).

There is a whole range of cultural issues that impact on customer relations that an organization needs to consider if expansion into another area of the world is being proposed. These include:

» what form of hierarchies does the culture encourage;
» attitudes to gender;
» attitudes to age and experience;

» who makes buying decisions; and
» what is acceptable and not acceptable in advertising copy.

## GLOBAL PRODUCTS

It has already been mentioned in this material that the same types of products and services are now available on a global basis. However as George S Yip points out in *Total Global Strategy* (1992), the idea of a completely similar product/service available all over the globe is a myth. There are nearly always local variations as a result of differences and culture. At the simplest level these may be purely linguistic. Coca-Cola is one of the most standardized global products but even Coke labels need to reflect the language of the user. It is noticeable that many products now include multi-lingual labels and instruction. Even mundane products such as shower gel on sale in the UK may include labels with English, French, Portuguese, Italian etc. lettering on the same label in an attempt to cut costs.

It is vitally important that effective market research is carried out to see whether changes need to be made to a standard product. There may well be legislative reasons for doing so. Whilst automobiles now look very similar in most countries, governments have different safety and emission regulations and these need to be catered for. Not all countries drive on the right hand side of the road. The UK, Ireland, India and Pakistan, Cyprus, Australia, New Zealand, and a part of the US (the US Virgin Islands) still drive on the left. Modern manufacturing techniques have made it easier to produce left and right hand drive automobiles using the same jigs, machine tools and production lines but the issue also affects headlight lenses etc. - small points but very important ones.

There may be demographic differences. A product that is dominated by sales to female customers in one culture may be more male oriented in another; small automobiles are a good example. Something that appeals to youth in one place may be initially more attractive to an older age range in another. The mobile telephone market started with the business sector as the main customers with domestic customers entering the market later on.

McDonald's has become famous for both a highly standardized product and a highly standardized level of service and delivery, but even they make local adaptations. Islamic and Jewish cultures do not eat pork whilst the French expect alcohol to be served in such establishments whilst people in the UK do not. Within the standardized product, McDonald's has been able to cater for local variations. The knowledge that such variations are necessary at the outset of an expansion can greatly aid in building a loyal customer base.

It may be necessary to change the name of a product to suit local customer preferences although the current trend is to adopt names that are culturally neutral thus allowing the same name to be used globally. Many of the automobile producers actually make names up, the Ford Ka being an example, or use numbers or a word that is clearly recognized globally, Mondeo, Neon etc. The UK brand name of the confectionery Snickers was for a long time Marathon until it was realized that UK purchasers would accept the Snickers name. Organizations need to be very careful that what is acceptable in one language is not unacceptable in another. Both of the two major airframe manufacturers in the world, Boeing and Airbus Industrie, use numbers for their products e.g. Boeing 777 or Airbus A340 thus avoiding any problems with names.

Even if the product stays the same, the packaging may change to reflect local culture. Pictures of Caucasian children on a product destined for Asia would be insensitive. US and UK Cornflakes taste the same – the packaging is similar but not quite the same. Kellogg's has managed to achieve what Coca-Cola has also managed–many in the UK think that Kellogg's Cornflakes are a UK product. Perhaps the true indicator of having "gone global" is that people in a particular market believe that the product/service/brand is indigenous to that market.

According to Yip there are only 19 truly global brands, the top five of which are: Coca-Cola, Sony, Mercedes Benz, Kodak, and Disney. Apparently nearly everybody in the world knows about and recognizes these names. Not surprisingly Levi-Strauss, Kellogg's, and Ford are also in the list.

## BEST PRACTICE

### Kalmbach Publishing (US)

Kalmbach Publishing is a US publisher and distributor of high-quality consumer and trade magazines and books covering hobby, special interest, and leisure-time subjects as well as a sponsor of consumer shows. Located in Brookfield, Wisconsin, Kalmbach publications cater not just for US and Canadian readers but also interested consumers across the globe.

The company grew considerably in the latter part of the twentieth century. In 1985 Kalmbach published three magazines and employed 70 people. By 2002 the company publishes 14 magazines, has over 250 books in print (plus ancillary products), and employs nearly 300 people.

On 15 December 1933, Albert C. Kalmbach posed for a photograph with the 272 copies of the first issue of *Model Railroader* magazine. 1933 was a difficult time for the US and other economies and, unable to obtain employment, Kalmbach, whose hobbies and interests included printing and model trains, decided to launch a magazine catering to other model railroad enthusiasts. By 2002 the Kalmbach company is still a major name in the railroad associated interests market not just in the US and Canada but also in many other parts of the world.

Despite the difficult economic times, *Model Railroader* was joined in 1940 by another title – *Trains*. It concentrated on real (as opposed to model) railroading. With the end of hostilities in 1945 Kalmbach Publishing rapidly built up a line of hobby books and investigated other opportunities.

In 1982 the growth in plastic scale-model kits encouraged the company to commence publication of *FineScale Modeler*, now the hobby's leading publication.

The company broadened its scope in 1985 by acquiring the Astro-Media Corporation, another Milwaukee publisher, whose flagship publication was *Astronomy*. Yet another acquisition, in 1987, brought *Dollhouse Miniatures* (formerly *Nutshell News*) and *Model Retailer* into the Kalmbach family.

Responding to the growing nostalgia-related market of the late 1980s, Kalmbach introduced *Classic Toy Trains* (1987), a start-up that quickly found a large and appreciative audience not just in the US and Canada but also in Europe of which the UK was an important market.

In July 1989, after 43 years at the same downtown Milwaukee location in which the first magazine was produced, the company moved to new quarters in suburban Brookfield.

Kalmbach bought Greenberg Publishing and Greenberg Shows in 1991, later integrating Greenberg's publishing operation with Kalmbach's own. Greenberg Shows sponsors about 40 shows annually for those who collect model trains and collectible toys. Whilst other countries such as the UK and Germany have a tradition of model railway exhibitions, these are organized by local enthusiasts, there being little in Europe to match the commercial sponsorship provided by Greenberg.

Expansion into a different market occurred in 1995 when Kalmbach acquired *Birder's World*, a magazine for both casual bird watchers and serious birders. A year later three new magazines were added to the Kalmbach list – *Garden Railways*, *Scale Auto*, and *Bead & Button*.

2000 saw the launch of *Classic Trains* and the acquisition of *The Writer* and *Plays* magazines.

A long-term program of converting magazine and book production to digital workflow began in 1995 and culminated in going computer-to-plate with all titles in 1999. The company established an on-line publishing department in 1997, and each magazine has a Website on the Internet.

With 14 popular magazines and a broad line of hobby books Kalmbach is an important name in the hobby market.

Model railways have come a long way since the crude representations of the 1930s. Modern model locomotives can cost hundreds of dollars and the worth of many collections is well into the thousands of dollars. Those spending such sums look to the magazines that support the hobby to be useful sources of information.

*Model Railroader*, dealing as it does with US and Canadian prototypes might be thought to have a market in only those two countries. However there are many modelers in the rest of the world. There are a number of national magazines that cater for those modeling prototypes along with their own national railway systems. In the UK the main model-railroading magazine, *Railway Modeler*, has a companion publication–*Continental Modeler*–that covers prototypes from the rest of the world including the US and Canada. Iain Rice, regular contributor to Kalmbach's railway publications in the US, is based firmly in the UK where he models and writes about UK as well as North American prototypes. Recognizing that there is a large overseas market,

Kalmbach ensures that their overseas customers receive the same high quality of service as those customers in the US and Canada. All of the publications are in English and the majority of overseas customers are English speakers. Using a credit card and accessing Kalmbach either by telephone or the Internet an overseas customer can set up and pay for the magazines he or she requires for periods ranging from 12 though 36 months. The longer the subscription is prepaid the higher the discount.

Communication with the company is easy (although it is necessary to remember that the company may well be in a different time zone to that of the customer) as each magazine has a full list of contact information. The magazines are delivered well packaged and there is little time lag between the current month's issue appearing on US bookstands and popping through the mailbox of a reader in the UK.

One of the concerns of foreign customers is what happens if there is non-delivery. Not only are Kalmbach staff extremely friendly and efficient but a replacement copy is sent with alacrity.

The only Kalmbach feature that cannot be accessed by foreign customers is in the field of competitions where US legislation on sweepstakes etc. prohibits the involvement of non-residents. In all other respects the customer care provided by Kalmbach is exactly the same as for the US/Canadian customer.

The magazines, especially those concerned with model railroading, provide detailed reviews of new products. Indigenous and foreign products suitable for modeling in either the historical or modern North American railroading scene are covered with equal fairness. These reviews are especially useful to foreign customers who may not see the products in their hobby shops for some time.

Whilst it might be thought that model railroading is an occupation for children this would be very far off the mark. The model railroader of the twenty-first century is willing to pay hundreds (and in some cases thousands) of dollars for a product. The technology includes computer design of layouts, computer control of equipment using digital command systems, and even video cameras attached to locomotives to give an engineer's view. Keeping customers across the world up to date with such developments is an important part of the relationship Kalmbach has with its subscribers wherever they live.

The Kalmbach products are about North American railroading etc., but are not purely aimed at North American modelers. The way articles are written provides for an explanation of terms that may be different to those used in other parts of the world.

Whilst model railroading may not seem a suitable subject for a business case study it is in fact a multi-billion dollar industry with adherents all over the globe. The international nature of *Model Railroader* was evidenced in the fall of 2001 when there were letters published in the magazine from railroad modelers across the globe expressing their shock and stating their support for their US colleagues in the wake of the terrorist attacks on Washington DC and New York on September 11 of that year.

As the technology of publishing changed so Kalmbach has changed with it. This has meant that Kalmbach has been able to take advantage of the universal nature of hobbies to continually develop products with global appeal that act as a binding agent for those from different nations and cultures who share a particular leisure interest.

## KALMBACH PUBLISHING TIMELINE

- » **1933**: Albert C. Kalmbach starts *Model Railroader*.
- » **1934**: *Trains* magazine started.
- » **1935**: Staff: 70; magazines: 3. AstroMedia Corp. acquired.
- » **1936**: *Dollhouse Miniatures* and *Model Retailer* acquired. *Classic Toy Trains* first published.
- » **1937**: New HQ opened.
- » **1938**: Greenberg Publications and Shows acquired.
- » **1939**: *Birder's World* acquired.
- » **1940**: *Garden Railways*, *Scale Auto* and *Bead and Button* published.
- » **1941**: *Classic Trains* launched. *The Writer* and *Plays* magazines acquired.
- » **1982**: First issue of *FineScale Modeler*.
- » **1997**: On-line publishing started.
- » **2002**: Staff: 300; magazines: 14; book titles: 250.

## KEY LEARNING POINTS

» When operating in a global marketplace organizations need to understand customer concerns regarding payments and complaints.

» Organizations can only develop a good relationship with foreign customers if they take cultural differences into account.

» Global success is best achieved by "thinking globally but acting locally."

» Organizations such as Kalmbach have thought through how to attract and retain their overseas customer base.

# Customer Relations:

# the State of the Art

This chapter considers the current state of the art in respect of customer relations. It explains how:

» not all customers are good customers;
» mere satisfaction is often not enough to engender loyalty;
» delighting the customer and repeat business should be key objectives;
» the customer accumulator operates;
» the types of loyalty that customers can display; and
» the fact that loyalty cannot be guaranteed.

David Clutterbuck and Walter Goldsmith in *The Winning Streak Mk II*, (1997), a follow up to their 1985 text *The Winning Streak*, make four very important points that impact on the current state of the art of customer relations. They state that:

» the best customer is usually an existing customer;
» organizations should focus on developing a talent for focusing on the customers the organization really wants to keep;
» it is critical to build firm relationships with customers; and
» competitive advantage should be given a higher priority than cost.

Not every customer is a good customer. Every organization probably has "folklore" relating to those customers that they do not want. Such customers may be bad payers, rude or expect far too much for what they are prepared to pay. Organizations may well decide to "fire" such customers. There is nothing wrong with this as a strategy provided that the organization realizes that the ex-customer may well go to a competitor and will almost certainly tell his or her friends about the negative experience he or she has had with the organization.

## SATISFACTION AND DELIGHT

Many organizations can satisfy their customers but it is only those organizations prepared to put the customer at the very center of their operations that are able to delight the customer. Satisfaction is better than dissatisfaction but even the use of the word in English suggests that there is far more that could be achieved. Satisfaction is only a partial step on the road to delight.

Later on in this chapter when customer loyalty is considered it will be shown that it is not satisfaction but delight that secures long-term loyalty. In emotive terms satisfaction is what the customer expects, delight is what provides a warm glow. Delight, from the customer's point of view, could be described as receiving more than the minimum expected added value. Delighting a customer actually adds added value to the continuing relationship between the supplier and the customer.

## CUSTOMER RELATIONS AND THE FINANCIAL BOTTOM LINE

Together with the price of stocks/shares, market share is an important measure of an organization's performance, one that is accorded considerable weight by investors.

As the writer of this material demonstrated in 2000, the effect of a loss of customers to a rival is not a simple arithmetic progression but follows what he described as the "customer accumulator."

Imagine a situation where there are two retail outlets in a town, both selling similar items (see Table 6.1). Initially each has 100 customers. For the purpose of this exercise it is assumed that the total customer base will remain at 200. Examine the effect of outlet B gaining 1, 2, 10, 25 and 50 customers from Outlet A. Outlet A has lost half its customers but it is now three times smaller and thus perhaps three times less attractive to investors than Outlet B. Assume, for the purpose of this exercise, that each customer generates $10 of profit (see Table 6.2). Not only is Outlet B now three times bigger in terms of market share, it is also three times more profitable and the comparison of profitability is a key ratio in deciding the relative strength and success of organizations.

One of the most useful definitions of an effective organization is "One that listens to its customers and then meets their needs at an acceptable cost to both parties" (Cartwright & Green, 1997).

Outlet B is clearly more effective than outlet A.

**Table 6.1** The customer accumulator (adapted from Cartwright R, 2000, *Mastering Customer Relations*).

| Outlet A customers | Outlet A market share | Outlet B customers | Outlet B market share | Numerical difference B − A | Relative size of B compared to A |
|---|---|---|---|---|---|
| 100 | 50% | 100 | 50% | 0 | equal |
| 99 | 49.5% | 101 | 50.5% | 2 | 1.02 |
| 98 | 49% | 102 | 51% | 4 | 1.04 |
| 90 | 45% | 110 | 55% | 20 | 1.2 |
| 75 | 37.5% | 125 | 62.5% | 50 | 1.6 |
| 50 | 25% | 150 | 75% | 100 | 3 |

**Table 6.2** The effect of the customer accumulator on profit.

| Outlet A Customers | Outlet A Profit | Outlet B Customers | Outlet B Profit |
|---|---|---|---|
| 100 | $1000 | 100 | $1000 |
| 99 | $990 | 101 | $1010 |
| 98 | $980 | 102 | $1020 |
| 90 | $900 | 110 | $1100 |
| 75 | $750 | 125 | $1250 |
| 50 | $500 | 150 | $1500 |

## LOYALTY

Yoram J. Wind (1982) examined customer loyalty and postulated that there are five classifications of customers or potential customers in respect of loyalty.

1 Current loyal customers who will continue to use the product or service.
2 Current customers who may switch to another brand.
3 Occasional customers who would increase consumption of the brand if the incentive were right.
4 Occasional customers who would decrease consumption of the brand if a competitor offered the right incentive.
5 Non-users who could become customers.

There is also a final category that can be described as non-customers as they are:

6 Non-users who will never become customers.

Within customer/potential customer categories one to five it is important to distinguish between loyalty to the generic product, the brand, and a particular supplier.

Many people are loyal to coffee as a beverage. There are also those who are only occasional coffee drinkers and those who never drink coffee at all, perhaps for medical or religious reasons. Those who drink considerable amounts of coffee can be described as having a generic product loyalty. Within that group there will be some that buy just the cheapest coffee or drink whatever is available. For them the writer

(2000) introduced the term "a-loyal." They are loyal to the generic product but not to a particular brand. They are not disloyal, as that implies that there has been a loyalty to a particular brand at some time. Later in this chapter these brand a-loyal customers will be equated to a type of customer known as a mercenary.

Within the group of those who are product loyal there will be those who have a particular brand loyalty. They always buy a particular brand such as Maxwell House or Nescafe or at least a brand from the same producer. According to Alsop (1989) who studied brand loyalty in the USA, cigarettes, mayonnaise and toothpaste carried a 60 percent brand loyalty, while plastic bags and tinned vegetables had very little brand loyalty. The situation has become more complicated as retail suppliers such as the large supermarkets have begun to introduce their own brands at a price usually much lower than that of the better-known brands in order to appeal to supplier loyalty rather than brand loyalty.

## SUPPLIER LOYALTY

Many customers are creatures of habit. Not only are they loyal to particular brands, there is also a loyalty to particular suppliers. The work on customer behavior to be covered later in this chapter introduces a type of customer known as a hostage, i.e. somebody who has no choice but to be a customer of a particular brand or supplier. Such a situation could occur in a small community where there is only one shop selling perhaps just one brand of a particular item. A customer who is without transport could be forced, if they really want the item, to be loyal to that one brand and that one supplier. The term the writer introduced for this is "pseudo-loyalty." A statistical analysis of the customer base would show considerable loyalty but it is mere pseudo-loyalty, because given the opportunity the customer might well choose another brand from another supplier. The introduction of large edge-of-town supermarkets throughout the world has provided a dramatic illustration of pseudo-loyalty as smaller shops see customers they had previously thought of as extremely loyal defecting to the supermarkets in large numbers lured by lower prices and increased choice.

## SUPRA-LOYALTY

Supra-loyalty is a term that can be used to describe people who are extremely loyal to an organization, product or service. In the case of loyalty to an organization they have normally built up a personal relationship with it over a period of time, or in the case of a product/service they identify themselves with it. It is as if they have internalized the relationship and consider themselves almost part of the organization instead of being a customer.

Supra-loyalty can obviously be very beneficial to an organization as its customers actually perform a marketing function for it by telling their friends, relations and colleagues about it. However if the customer becomes disillusioned then he or she may well tell friends, family and colleagues about their dissatisfaction – a type of publicity no organization needs.

## DE-LOYALTY

A customer who makes a deliberate decision to move to another organization because he or she has been let down by an organization that they were previously loyal to can be described as being "de-loyal." This is not the same as disloyalty, which suggests that it is the customer who is doing something wrong. In the case of de-loyalty it is the organization that has let the customer down.

There is evidence that people are willing to forgive one mistake or one case of poor service provided that rectification of the situation (and an apology) is speedily forthcoming. However if a supra-loyal customer becomes disenchanted they may take their business elsewhere, in effect becoming de-loyal. If they are very, very disappointed they may become "anti-loyal" and seek retribution against the organization, becoming what are known as terrorists, a phenomenon that will be covered later in this chapter.

Sales staff who have front-line contact with the customer need to be empowered to rectify problems as quickly and as easily as possible. The longer a customer has to wait, or the harder he or she has to fight for a resolution to a problem, the more de-loyal he or she is likely to become. Early resolution strengthens the bonds of loyalty as it shows that the organization cares about the customer.

## DISLOYALTY

It is a moot point as to whether a customer can actually be disloyal. Customers owe nothing in terms of loyalty to suppliers. Whilst many customers may feel that they are being disloyal if they go elsewhere, feeling disloyal is not the same as being disloyal. The only obligation actually placed on a customer is to render payment for the product or service provided whether the payment is in monetary or other terms.

Organizations, however, carrying as they do a responsibility to their customers, can be disloyal. Disloyalty from an organization is deliberately not providing a product or service to a previously loyal customer. An example of this would be an organization that treated a new customer better, deliberately or not, than an existing customer. In this case the organization would be being disloyal to the relationship that had been built up. If the existing customer decided to go elsewhere then they would be making a perfectly valid and proper decision.

## CUSTOMER BEHAVIOR

This chapter has introduced a number of terms that can be used to describe the degree of loyalty a customer has to a particular generic product, brand or supplier: a-loyal, supra-loyal, de-loyal, pseudo-loyal and anti-loyal. In effect they describe a variety of customer behaviors. Work by Jones and Sasser in the USA has also considered customer loyalty and in particular why apparently satisfied customers defect to another supplier or product. The answer is that mere satisfaction is no longer enough for an increasing number of customers. As quality and choice increase, delight becomes the customer goal rather than just satisfaction.

Unless they are a-loyal, delighted customers do not defect unless they cease to become delighted or are even more delighted by the offering of a competitor.

The bonds of loyalty become strengthened over time as each good experience builds on the previous one. This means that a competitor will need to provide considerably more delight in order to woo a customer and that may well not be a cost effective method of gaining new customers.

Jones and Sasser make the point that many organizations believe that if their customer feedback mechanisms indicate satisfaction then the organization is in a good position. Their research however showed a weak link between satisfaction and loyalty. As products and services improve then satisfaction becomes in effect the minimum acceptable standard. Just as the terms supra-loyalty and pseudo-loyalty were introduced earlier so Jones and Sasser have referred to long-term loyalty and false loyalty.

Jones and Sasser have concluded that as soon as there is increased competition then the level of satisfaction required to retain previously loyal customers increases. They point out that whilst in monopoly/oligopoly situations the customer has restricted choice. But as soon as competition opens out it is the supplier who has only one real choice. They must provide existing customers with higher and higher levels of satisfaction. The easier it becomes to switch, the more likely it is to happen.

Many banks throughout the world have made a point of targeting students to open accounts with them despite the fact that students have little if any disposable income during their time at college or university. The fact is that graduates are likely to earn more over their working lives than non-graduates and thus provide more business and revenue for their bank. In the past people displayed a reluctance to switch to another bank regardless of the level of service offered by their current bank. Part of this may be due to loyalty but it has also been relatively complicated to switch to another bank. Banks are now making it much easier for customers to change to them by easing the complexities that the customer could experience. This is of course a two edged sword. If you make it easier for somebody to switch from a competitor to you, your competitors will make it easier for your customers to defect to them.

Similar issues relate to changing one's e-mail and Internet service provider (ISP), as this may require a new e-mail address. People will have to be informed and so it is easier to remain with the current provider even if the service levels are not as good as those of a competitor. There appears to be a threshold of service below which customers will switch, but above which they are reluctant to move no matter what inducements the competitor makes.

When the UK government deregulated telephones, gas and electricity in the 1990s the various suppliers made it relatively simple for customers to switch provision. British Telecom, as the UK market leader for telephone services, also made it easy and cheap for defectors to return.

The importance of total satisfaction (or delight) against mere satisfaction was demonstrated by the example of the reprographics giant, Xerox, as profiled by Jones and Sasser (1995). They found that delighted Xerox customers were a staggering six times more likely to give repeat business to Xerox than merely satisfied customers. As it is unlikely to cost six times more to delight a customer than to merely satisfy him or her, then the financial advantages of delighting the customer seem self evident.

Jones and Sasser have developed terminology for six types of customer behavior that can be linked closely to the types of loyalty discussed earlier.

## Apostles

Apostles demonstrate supra-loyalty. The apostle is delighted with the service or product and, as stated earlier when considering supra-loyalty, may actually identify with the organization or the product. This is of course good news for any organization. Apostles in effect carry out a marketing function for the organization. They are highly loyal and delighted and they tell their friends and relations.

But there are downsides to having a large number of apostles in the customer base. Their identification with the organization may be so close that they can come to believe that they are actually part of the organization. When this happens the distance that should rightly be present in the customer–supplier relationship is destroyed and the apostle can become a nuisance by demanding special treatment and interfering in matters that are really not their concern such as internal arrangements that have no effect on the customer. In effect they can become a bad customer.

The biggest danger associated with the apostle is the tendency to become highly disruptive if dissatisfied. Apostles are paradoxically the most fertile source of the organization's worst enemy, the terrorist. It is said that "Hell hath no fury like a woman scorned" but to an organization "Hell hath no fury to compare to a highly dissatisfied apostle." The dissatisfied apostle does not just feel let down. Because of their perceived close link to the organization they can feel betrayed and with betrayal may come a wish for revenge and retribution.

Apostles are unlikely to switch unless they become very dissatisfied, but when they do it will be in such a manner as not to go unnoticed. There have been instances of previously very loyal customers to an auto dealership becoming dissatisfied with a purchase and after failing to achieve satisfaction parking the offending vehicles outside the dealership with a notice prominently displayed drawing attention to their complaints. A recent phenomenon has been for dissatisfied customers to set up Websites attacking the organization that has incurred their wrath.

David Harvey (2002) has spoken of turning occasional customers into evangelists by responding to the power shift from supplier to customer (especially by exploiting the Internet) and changing to a customer focused operation. He points out that legislation and social pressures are favoring customers more and more over suppliers and thus suppliers need to respond in order to survive.

## Loyalists

Loyalists form the most important component of the customer base. They are akin to the "cash cows" described by the Boston Consulting Group to describe those products that form the basis for organizational success. Loyalists require much less effort on their behalf than apostles, yet are very loyal customers coming back time and again. They tend to be less volatile than apostles are and thus more tolerant of mistakes. They are less voluble in their complaints but that does not mean that the organization can afford to ignore them. An organization that loses the support of its loyalists is on the downward spiral to major problems.

Whilst there might be a certain glamour attached to apostles and their effusive praise of an organization, loyalists are the true firm foundation for any customer base. Loyalists provide the stability and objectivity required for sustained growth. Loyalists form useful members of focus groups as they will not be afraid to tell the truth as they see it but they will be objective in doing so and that will provide useful data for the organization.

Jones and Sasser make the point that loyalists are the easiest customers to deal with. This is true, but customers only become loyalists as a result of high quality products and services being delivered to them over a period of time, and when there have been complaints, they have been rectified expeditiously. Loyalty, as stressed earlier, does not occur at a single point in time but is built up over a series of successful interactions.

## Mercenaries

Mercenaries are the hardest customers to deal with, as they are a-loyal. Mercenaries go for the cheapest or the most convenient option. They are difficult to deal with because they may well be satisfied and even delighted but they are not loyal. Mercenaries may be brand loyal but supplier a-loyal. They may well move from brand to brand or supplier to supplier. If asked why they moved the answer may be in terms of cost or convenience but it may well be just a desire for a change.

The problem for an organization is whether to expend energy or indeed money on trying to turn a mercenary into a loyalist. The organization will need to satisfy the mercenary even if no repeat business is expected as they will tell people about bad products and services. Unless they are very delighted it may well be that they will continue to shop around. From the organization's point of view it is important not to pander too much to the mercenary. Too big a discount on the first transaction may well mean that they will always want such levels if they return – but they are just as likely to go down the road and quote your discount to a competitor in the hope that it will be bettered. The problem of course is that the mercenary is difficult to spot during the first transaction. It is only when they re-appear that their nature becomes apparent.

## Hostages

Hostages appear to be very loyal but that is only because they have no choice. If a town only has one cinema then it will receive the vast majority of the cinema trade. An organization will not know whether its customers are loyalists or hostages until a competitor or a substitute enters the market.

Hostages have no choice; there is only one convenient shop, one local supplier, one hospital to go to etc. They have no choice but to demonstrate attributes of loyalty even when dissatisfied. Hence the use of the term pseudo-loyalty for this type of behavior.

The time for an organization to assess the loyalty and satisfaction of its customers is not when a competitor opens up; it is before then. If they are dissatisfied hostages will leave as soon as they have an opportunity. Even satisfied hostages may leave for a while in order to assess a new competitor. The original supplier will have to hope that the original product/service was of sufficient quality to tempt them back. It is too late to offer discounts and/or enhancements after competition starts. Hostages will ask, and rightly, why they were not offered them before.

The developments of e-commerce as discussed in Chapter 4 have provided those who were hostages with many more choices. If the world becomes one's shopping window for certain products and services then one is no longer a hostage for those products and services.

## Defectors

Dissatisfy even a loyalist often enough and they may well defect from the organization. Once a customer has defected and given their custom to another organization it may well be difficult to recover the situation, as they will begin to build up loyalty bonds with their new supplier or brand.

Organizations need to ensure that complaints are dealt with in an expeditious manner so that any temporary dissatisfaction does not become permanent and thus lead to defection. One organization's lost customer is a gain for a competitor, with the financial penalties as shown in the customer accumulator introduced earlier in this chapter. The defector displays characteristics of de-loyalty as discussed earlier.

Organizations that maintain close contacts with their customers may well witness defection at an early stage and be able to win the customer back. More and more suppliers maintain loyalty schemes that allow them to have regular contact with customers.

## Terrorists

The terrorist in customer relations terms is the worst nightmare an organization can have. Just as the political terrorist acknowledges no rules, neither, it appears, does the customer relations terrorist.

Terrorists may have been former apostles displaying supra-loyalty until they were let down and the situation was not recovered. They are not so much dissatisfied with the organization, product, or service as at war with it. They have a desire for revenge and retribution. Many of those who appear on consumer affairs television programs have been previous apostles. On being let down, they have no problem in letting the world know about it.

The longer a situation remains unresolved the angrier the terrorist becomes and sometimes their actions may be extreme, irrational, and even criminal. The threat of a court appearance for harassment or breach of the peace in respect of their relationship with an organization may well have an unexpected and negative effect. Court means publicity and by the time a customer becomes a terrorist, putting the problem right is no longer enough; they want to see the organization humiliated.

The best method of dealing with this type of terrorist is to do what should never be done to a political terrorist – give them what they want, more if necessary, and hope that they either become loyalists and apostles again or go away. The organization may consider concentrating on cutting its losses rather than trying to win back the custom. Terrorists are not de-loyal or even disloyal, they are anti-loyal; it is a case of love turning to hate.

Jones and Sasser's work is useful in that it provides an easy to understand explanation of why mere satisfaction is no longer enough to generate loyalty. Loyalty must be earned and should never be taken for granted. A summary of loyalty and satisfaction is shown in the loyalty matrix in Fig. 6.1.

## HOW CAN LOYALTY BE MEASURED?

This is a question that can only be answered in a situation where there is considerable choice available to the customer. Customers will be truly loyal and not displaying pseudo-loyalty when the quality and

| High | | |
|---|---|---|
| | HOSTAGE (PSEUDO-LOYAL) | APOSTLE (SUPRA-LOYAL) |
| LOYALTY | | LOYALIST (LOYAL) |
| | DEFECTOR (DE-LOYAL) | MERCENARY (A-LOYAL) |
| | TERRORIST (ANTI-LOYAL) | |
| Low | | |
| | Low | SATISFACTION | High |

**Fig. 6.1** The loyalty matrix.

value for money that they receive is sufficient for them to ignore the competition even when the competitor can offer either a slight cost saving, enhanced convenience, or both together.

## ORGANIZATIONAL BODY LANGUAGE

As part of the work for the book *In Charge of Customer Satisfaction* (1997), George Green introduced the term organizational body language (OBL). George and his co-author, the present writer, had discovered that it was not only individuals who signaled their true feelings through body language. Organizations also exhibited a form of body language that showed their true feelings about the customer.

Organizations can display as many mission statements and platitudes about their relationship with the customer as they like. It is the actual experience that the customer receives that will determine the strength of the customer–supplier relationship.

OBL relates to the whole atmosphere that an organization creates. There are organizations that clearly welcome the customer with open arms and there are those that may claim to but in fact the message the customer actually receives is one that seems to state that the customer is actually rather a nuisance who has to be tolerated!

It might seem strange that there would be organizations that do not positively welcome customers, but they abound. A typical example is the organization that has arranged its parking lot in such a manner that customers park at the end furthest from reception. The parking spaces next to the reception area are "reserved for company vehicles." A company mission statement claiming that customers come first will be of little consequence to a customer who has just walked from their car to reception in the pouring rain and passes the company parking spaces right next to the reception area.

An organization that has thought about OBL will have put the customer first; customer parking should be for the convenience of the customer and not the organization; reception will be easy to find – it will provide somewhere for the customer to sit with newspapers and magazines; there may even be a pot of coffee!

When the present writer and George Green were developing the OBL concept they found many, many examples of messages that send out negative OBL signals to the customer and give the impression that the organization thinks about itself first and the customer second. They are listed here with permission.

» There is no car parking space reserved for a customer who is expected.
» The customer arrives to find a locked door and no explanation. (The door may need to be locked for security reasons but the means of entry should be made clear to the customer.)
» There is nobody in reception.
» There is somebody there but they have their backs to the customer.
» There is somebody there but they walk off as the customer approaches.
» There are people there but they are interested in each other not the customer.
» There is a large queue and only one person is serving while others are walking about doing other things.
» There is loud music blaring.
» There is someone at reception but nowhere to sit and wait.
» Reception has never heard of the customer even though he or she has an appointment.
» No-one answers the telephone.

» The customer leaves a message on an answering machine and no-one calls back.
» No-one answers the customer's letters.
» The customer arrives in reception and no one has ever heard of the person the customer has arranged to see!

The last point may seem far-fetched but often happens when a new member of staff joins the company and nobody remembers to tell reception and the switchboard. OBL proactive organizations ensure that staff changes are notified to reception and the switchboard in advance with a note of the date and time they take effect.

Outstanding organizations will usually pay close attention to this organizational body language and ensure that the customer is not only told that they are important, but that the customer's experience will bear this out. It is a known fact that a good initial feeling leads to a "halo" effect whereby subsequent events are judged from a positive point of view. A bad start to a customer–supplier relationship can lead to a "horns" dilemma. For example, if the first few transactions between an organization and a customer are good and there is then a less than satisfactory transaction the customer is most likely to put the bad experience down to a temporary aberration - they have put a halo around the organization. If the first couple of transactions are less than satisfactory then, provided that the customer has not gone elsewhere, a subsequent good transaction may be thought of in terms of "well they managed to get it right that time but will it last?" The customer is on the horns of the dilemma as to which transactions really represent the organization. Should they defect anyway in case subsequent transactions follow the initial pattern?

Organizations have a perennial problem: one bad event can wipe out many good ones in an instant! With all interactions between an organization and its customers the halo/horns effect will apply. If the organization is open and welcoming customers will assume that this reflects the rest of the organization (halo). If it is the opposite (horns) then they will assume the worst.

Organizations need to be aware that there is an aural version of the halo/horns effect. If customers or potential customers overhear someone talking about an organization this is likely to influence them. Staff need to be aware that if they are wearing company identification, any comments that they make about their organization may have a halo/horns effect on any listeners.

Another very important aspect of organizational body language is communicating very negatively. This is often manifested in the extremely negative notices that organizations display.

» Don't lean on the counter
» No credit; no checks; no refunds
» Broken counts as sold
» Do not touch
» No pushchairs
» No food to be consumed on these premises
» No children
» No dogs
» No cameras
» Keep off
» No change for telephones
» No bags beyond this point.

There may be very valid reasons for the above strictures (the last one is clearly a security issue) but it is the manner in which they are communicated that sets the tone for the customer. Every one of the above would send a more positive message if the word please was included. The message would appear much more positive if some form of explanation was given.

» For security reasons please leave your bags with the attendant.
» Newly sown grass, please keep off.
» Dangerous area, please keep children away etc.

Customers who meet a barrage of prohibition notices are likely to interpret this as "Go away, you're too much trouble" and this is a very foolish message for any organization to send to customers and potential customers.

Organizational body language can even include the sense of smell. It is possible to purchase essences to place in air conditioning systems so that the smell of roasting coffee or baking bread can waft through a supermarket and trigger an autonomic reaction in the customers.

Having a pot of coffee sending its aroma through a property is a well-known ploy of those trying to sell their house!

OBL determines what an organization actually thinks about its customers as opposed to what it says its policy is. There is no point in an organization claiming to be family friendly if there are no facilities to change or feed babies and if the seats and counters are too high for children.

In considering the impact of OBL on customers, organizations need to consider a series of factors:

» location/buildings;
» security;
» convenience;
» communications; and
» ambience.

## KEY LEARNING POINTS

» Not all customers are good customers.
» The best customer is often an existing customer.
» Mere satisfaction is often not enough to engender loyalty – delight is what strengthens the bonds of loyalty.
» Loyalty comes in many forms.
» Hostages display pseudo-loyalty.
» Dissatisfied customers who have been very loyal may become terrorists.
» Early resolution of problems strengthens loyalty.
» Never neglect an existing customer in order to gain or impress a new one.
» Loyalty can never be guaranteed.
» Organizational body language reflects what the organization really feels about its customers.

# Customer Relations Success Stories

This chapter contains three case studies of organizations that have demonstrated effective customer relations by delighting their customers.

The first case study chronicles the move of the commercial airliner division of Boeing from a product led to a customer driven orientation. The second considers the UK company Saga, an organization providing vacations and other products to the over 50s market. The third case study examines the Chowking Food Corporation in the Philippines.

Here we take a look at three case studies of organizations that have demonstrated effective customer relations. All three organizations have demonstrated a commitment to not only satisfying, but delighting their customers' needs and wants.

## BOEING – FROM PRODUCT LED TO CUSTOMER DRIVEN

There can be few people on earth who have not heard of the Boeing Company in Seattle (WA). Today Boeing is perhaps best known to the general public for its family of civil jet airliners but to an earlier generation their best-known products were the B17 Flying Fortress and B29 Super Fortress bombers that made such an impact in World War II.

Despite its close relationship with the military Boeing can be said to have started the process of mass air travel with the introduction of the Boeing 247 in 1933. The 247 was a streamlined twin-engined monoplane that carried 10 passengers at 190 mph. On the insistence of Charles Monteith, the chief engineer at Boeing, capacity was not increased, as many in the company would have liked. Monteith argued for speed over capacity – a decision that was to prove damaging to the company. Monteith even argued – unsuccessfully – against fitting the aircraft with a toilet! One of the design faults of the 247 was a wing spar that went right through the cabin necessitating a step on each side of it.

At the time Boeing was part of a conglomerate that also included United Airlines and United were promised the first 60 aircraft off the production line. TWA (Trans World Airlines) were also in the market for a twin-engined monoplane and, being unable to purchase the 247 due to the priority given to United, approached the Douglas Aircraft Corporation.

TWA specified an aircraft carrying 12 passengers with a range of 1000 miles and a speed of 185 mph. The aircraft had also to be able to take off with a full load on one engine in case of an engine failure.

Douglas Aircraft listened to the customer. It was clear that capacity and comfort were more important than speed. Douglas produced the DC1 prototype that was developed into the DC2. The DC2 was a twin-engined airliner carrying 14 passengers at the speed and range specified by TWA. Internally it was more comfortable than the 247 as there was no wing spar intruding into the passenger cabin. The airline bought 20 DC2s. Altogether Douglas sold 138 DC2s to airlines that were delighted with a product that stemmed from their needs rather than a designer's assumption.

Douglas Aircraft carried on development, and in 1935 produced the famous DC3 (Dakota) an aircraft that not only helped the allied victory in World War II (for which it was the main transport aircraft, even serving in Vietnam as a gunship) but also took Boeing out of the commercial airliner market as a major player for a generation.

By 1940 there were over 300 DC3s in airline service (including United). In 1944 the DC3 was the largest component in the Douglas sales total of $1,061,407,485 for that year. The DC3 and its successors saw Douglas gain the major market share for airliners outside the Soviet bloc until 1955. In the early years after World War II the DC3 formed the major item of equipment for the world's airlines. By the mid 1960s, however, Douglas was in dire financial problems and was forced into a merger with McDonnell.

Whilst Douglas had been building the DC3 and its successors, Boeing had been developing a series of bombers for the USAF. The B47 and the B52 (the latter still in service in 2002) gave Boeing considerable experience in the behavior of large multi-engined jet aircraft operating at high speed.

A tanker aircraft designed to support the B52 bomber was introduced and developed into the famous Boeing 707 – the world's first commercially successful jet airliner (the British Comet was earlier but lacked the capacity, speed and range of the 707 and had fatigue problems).

Boeing soon gained a major market share of the jet airliner market with versions of the 707, the smaller 727 and the 747 Jumbo Jet that entered commercial service in January 1970. Boeing had worked with Pan Am to develop the 747 and before long there were orders from the world's major airlines.

In the 1990s McDonnell Douglas ceased to be a major force in the airliner market (eventually becoming part of the Boeing empire) but across the Atlantic Airbus Industrie (a pan-European manufacturer) was gaining market share. There is a case study on Airbus Industrie in *Strategies for Hypergrowth*, a companion text in the ExpressExec series.

Airlines claimed that Boeing was ceasing to listen to what they wanted whereas Airbus did.

It was clear in the late 1980s that an aircraft larger than the twin-engined Boeing 767 introduced in 1982 but slightly smaller than the 747 was a requirement for many airlines. Airbus was developing the A330 (twin-engined) and the structurally similar A340 (four engines) to fill this gap in the market. Boeing continued to talk to the airlines about a stretched version of the 767.

As Karl Sabbach has commented in his 1995 text *21st Century Jet* it took some time before Boeing realized that airlines did not want a stretched 767 but a brand new design. For Boeing a new version of the 767 would be much easier to produce than a completely new design.

When Boeing realized that a new version of the 767 would not gain the desired market share the company moved from a product led approach to a customer driven one very quickly.

Prior to developing the new design (the Boeing 777) the airframe manufacturers produced a design and then "sold" it to the airlines. This approach had been undertaken for many years. Whilst customer comments were taken into account there had been some spectacular failures in the industry caused by designers not developing the products the customer really wanted. The UK could have scooped a major share of the market that later went to the Boeing 727 with the Trident Airliner. Many airlines were interested but only the version required by British European Airlines was built and that was slightly too small for other potential customers. Hawker Siddeley (later British Aerospace) was not prepared to develop a larger version and this allowed Boeing to sell over 1800 727s compared with a mere 117 Tridents.

For the new design, the Boeing 777, Boeing took the almost unprecedented step of inviting eight of their major customers to become involved in the design of the new model *without the invited airlines having to make a commitment to buy*. The airlines were:

» United, American, and Delta from the US;
» British Airways from Europe;
» Nippon and Japan Air Lines from Japan;
» Cathay Pacific from Hong Kong; and
» Qantas from Australia.

By choosing a global spread of customers Boeing was able to address cultural as well as technical issues.

Involving non-committed customers carries a risk that proprietary knowledge and plans will leak into the general marketplace but Boeing was confident that this was the right step to take. The potential customers were involved in quite detailed planning on the features of the new design. The planning stage lasted over 12 months and at the end of it Boeing was confident that the 777 was an aircraft that the customers wanted rather than a design that had been worked up and then needed to be sold to market.

That the decision to involve the potential customers in detailed design was correct was shown when United and British Airlines became the launch customers for the 777. By 2002 only Qantas out of the eight airlines involved was not an operator of the 777.

The Boeing 777 program was also unique in the degree of detailed involvement of subcontractors. Boeing used computer technology to link designers and contractors and all concerned parties in an issue were members of the relevant design build team (DBT). The operation of the Boeing Design Build Team features in the ExpressExec text, *Going Global.*

The airline industry in general was heavily affected by the tragic events of September 11, 2001. By keeping close to its customers Boeing stands a better chance of surviving the downturn in air travel that followed those tragic events than if it was still operating a product led approach.

## TIME LINE: BOEING

» **1917**: Boeing Company founded.
» **1918**: B1 – Boeing's first commercial aircraft developed.
» **1927**: Name changed to United Aircraft and Transportation Corporation – included Boeing, United Airlines, and the engine manufacturer Pratt & Whitney.
» **1933**: United Air Transportation broken up under US anti-trust legislation.
B247 developed. DC1 developed.
» **1934**: B17 Flying Fortress prototype developed.
» **1942**: First flight of B29 Super Fortress.

» **1947**: B47 jet bomber developed.
» **1951**: B52 bomber developed. Dash 80 the prototype for both the Stratotanker and the B707 developed.
» **1957**: B707 enters service.
» **1970**: B747 enters service.
» **1978**: B767 production starts.
» **1990**: Planning for B777 starts.
» **1995**: B777 enters service. Boeing and McDonnell Douglas merge.

**KEY INSIGHTS**

» The earlier a customer is involved in the design stage of a product the more likely the product is to reflect the customer's needs.
» Involving customers in design risks information leaking out but this is outweighed by the benefits of having a product that meets customer needs.
» Once a lead has been lost it may be very difficult to regain it.
» Involved customers are likely to be repeat customers.

**SAGA**

The gray market in this case study is the market for goods and services for older members of society (those whose hair is going or has gone gray). Whilst many companies have sought to exploit and expand into the youth market there is an increasing awareness that the gray market is also well worth examining.

As patterns of living and work have changed so has the relationship between the age groups. Many people are either retiring early to enjoy leisure activities or to seek a career change. There is also less pressure on parents to provide an inheritance for their children especially where the latter are in well-paid posts. A T-shirt on sale in recent years expresses the new relationship quite well with the slogan "I'm on vacation spending my kids' inheritance" on the back. The front read: "Old age and treachery will always overcome youth and inexperience" – a sentiment that is quite an interesting reflection of the way society is changing. Whilst the West may be accused of ignoring its more elderly members this is not true of other parts of the world where age and experience are revered.

In more and more parts of the world the gray market has increasing disposable income and many seem intent on spending a fair proportion of their wealth while they can still enjoy it.

In 1951, in Folkestone (UK) Sidney De Haan realized that retired people would appreciate the opportunity to take lower cost seaside vacations outside of the main vacation periods. The main vacation periods coincide with school vacations and thus hoteliers etc. offer discounts for those who vacation outside of the busiest periods. The first vacation De Haan offered cost $10.40 (£6.50) and included full board, travel to the resort and three excursions. While $10 went a lot further in 1951, the vacations were still a bargain.

Many in the vacation business scoffed at De Haan's decision to target a particular niche market. These vacations became more and more popular and the ability (at the time) to travel on day trips between the UK and France without a passport led De Haan to fly to Le Touquet in France from 1959. This was at a time when most British vacationers took their breaks at UK resorts and when few had actually traveled by aircraft.

So successful was this first foreign endeavor that in the 1960s De Haan pioneered tourism in the Algarve, establishing the Aldeia do Mar Turistica Holiday Complex at Albufeira.

Saga's customer base grew rapidly and in 1966 the Saga Club was launched with members receiving *Saga News*, the forerunner to the current *Saga Magazine*. At the time the age criteria for booking a Saga vacation was 60 – the age that females received the UK state pension (men received their pensions at 65). By the start of the 1970s Saga was also offering vacations to Romania, Spain and Yugoslavia with a US operation based in Boston (MA) commencing in 1979. By the end of 1981 US seniors were able to enjoy a Saga vacation.

As Sidney De Haan retired in 1984, *Saga Magazine* had been launched, providing general information and articles to those over 60. His son Roger took over the company and continued the tradition of finding out exactly what it was that the over 60 market required from their vacations. It has been this customer centered approach that has been the main reason for Saga's continuing success and growth.

The older members of society have always been amongst the safest drivers and have a reputation for being concerned about financial probity. In 1987 Saga Services was established to provide insurance, investment and other services for Saga customers. The Saga Magazine had become one of the UK's highest circulation magazines showing that Sidney De Haan was perfectly correct in deciding to provide his company's services to a niche market. As the number of older people has been growing steadily, it was in fact a very sensible market to target.

In 1988 Saga received its second Queen's Award for Export.

With the change in employment patterns and more and more people taking early retirement the qualifying age was lowered from 60 to 50 in 1995 thus opening up a much larger potential market.

Research carried out by the writer and his colleague Carolyn Baird in 1999 showed that the older a vacationer was, the more safety and security were likely to feature as choice factors in booking a vacation. The Saga operation provides the customer with an escort for every vacation that the company offers. Many of the vacations are organized through established travel and vacation operators. Saga, however, also provides its own representative for the vacation thus giving the customer a Saga point of contact all the time they are away from home.

In 1996 Saga surprised the vacation industry with a bold development that forms the main detail of this case study. The cruise industry has long been a favorite vacation mode for older people. The modern cruise industry has diversified to offer products to all age ranges (for further details see the case study on the Carnival Corporation in the ExpressExec title *Managing Hypergrowth*. Believing that there was a large enough market for a cruise ship for the over 50s, Saga acquired the 24,500 grt *Sagafjord* from Cunard in 1996 and renamed the vessel *Saga Rose*.

Saga's requirements were for a ship of sufficient range to undertake an annual world cruise (retired people can afford to take the 100 days required to circumnavigate the globe), larger cabins than the industry norm and a good proportion of single cabins. The latter requirement is very important as many older people are on their own and cannot afford the huge single supplements charged by many vacation operators.

The Saga Rose product is designed around the needs of a customer base that is over 50 and comprises far more than just a cruise. *Saga Rose* undertakes cruises to the most popular cruising destinations for its predominantly but not exclusively UK clientele. In this respect Saga offers similar products to its main UK competitors for the middle price range cruise business, P&O and Cunard.

Recognizing that a main attraction for the over 50 age group is ease and security of travel Saga provides not only accommodation, food, and entertainment but also included in the price of the cruise is:

» travel insurance;
» all tips;
» standard class return rail fares or coach travel from the customer's home station to Dover or Southampton or to the airport for fly-cruises;
» private car service for customers living within 75 miles of the UK departure point; and
» for customers arriving by rail in London there is a coach from the main line terminals to the departure port or airport. Staff are present at the rail terminals to assist with baggage etc.

Saga also assists with currency purchases.

On-board payments made with Saga's own visa card attract a five per-cent discount.

At 24,500 grt *Saga Rose* carries 587 passengers and 350 crew. For comparison, the *Albatros* (a ship operating mainly in the German market) of similar tonnage carries over 1000 passengers and 10 less crew! *Saga Rose* has 63 dedicated single cabins whilst the *Albatros* has none. The Saga Rose product is more expensive but it is clear from the high level of bookings and the amount of repeat business that what is offered is regarded not only as value for money but also meets the needs of the customer base to a considerable degree of exactitude. In June of 2002 some of the accommodation for a cruise in December 2003 was already sold out.

Food and entertainment are designed to appeal to an older age range. The entertainment includes not only singers and comedians but also a number of specialist lecturers. Most cruise ships carry one or two specialist lecturers but *Saga Rose* often has as many as four on a cruise. This provides the customers with considerable choice as to how to fill their day. On a 2002 cruise up the coast of Norway and on to Longyearbyen (Spitzbergen) just 500 miles from the North Pole the passengers received lectures during the days at sea from the ex-editor of the *Guinness Book of Records*, an ex-reporter and explorer, a Norwegian specialist and a maritime historian. That learning never ceases was shown by the fact that members of the University of the Third Age, an organization dedicated to learning opportunities for the retired, was able to hold well-attended meetings on board the ship.

It is a fact that women tend to live longer than men, and thus there are likely to be more single females than males on the *Saga Rose*. Recognizing this, Saga is one of the few remaining cruise companies (Fred Olsen Lines is another) to provide two male dance hosts for the female customers.

Everything about the Saga Rose product seems to have been done with the needs and wants of the customer base in mind. Saga has taken great care to meet the needs of its customers, even down to the provision of food and beverage items that reflect the lifestyle of the customer.

There is no casino on *Saga Rose* but the ship does display a degree of comfort that one associates with a country house hotel or even one's own home. Comfort not glitz is perhaps more important after a certain time in life.

Some 530 senior Britons plus a few Americans and some other Europeans on a trip into the Arctic Circle shows that the gray market is not one to be dismissed. Companies such as Saga that can cater to the needs of such a customer base find that their efforts are rewarded with considerable loyalty.

Saga's cruise business is such that in 2002 it was announced that they were to increase capacity by chartering the 12,500 grt *Minerva* (built on the hull of an incomplete ex-Soviet spy ship) with accommodation for 352 passengers. The ship is to be renamed *Saga Pearl* and will be operated to the same high standard as *Saga Rose*. There is little doubt that Saga will continue in the cruise business.

Other Saga enterprises have grown. In 2000 Saga launched Prime-Time (the customer's Prime Time that is) digital radio and in October 2001 Saga 105.7FM hit the airwaves in the West Midlands of the UK.

The adage that life begins at 50 or whenever you want it to is demonstrated by the fact that

» Saga now takes far more people on holiday to Borneo than to Bournemouth (a traditional vacation resort on the South Coast of England).
» Saga offers a wide range of vacations, with some of the more adventurous tours particularly designed to appeal to more active travelers. Saga customers have (and in increasing numbers) taken opportunities to scuba dive in Mauritius, take a hot air balloon ride over the Masai Mara game reserve, live like a cowboy on a ranch in the US Wild West, or ride an elephant through the jungle in Thailand.

What Saga offers its customers is a product for their particular needs. During the course of research for this material the writer met a lady who had embarked with her husband on a Saga world cruise a couple of years ago only for the husband to be taken ill necessitating their flight home. Unfortunately he died in 2001. The lady was taking a *Saga Rose* cruise in 2002 and the writer wondered if this would not be too upsetting with the memories of the place where her husband was taken ill. It transpired that Saga had been so thoughtful and efficient in the way that they had assisted the couple in their return home and in the way they continued to check up on the husband's progress that the lady would not dream of taking a vacation with anybody else.

Whilst the Saga product may appear more expensive than others at first glance, the inclusion of travel to and from the vacation or ship and the inclusion of tips on *Saga Rose* means that the costs are all up front. Many older people surveyed found this preferable to a lower initial cost but then having to pay for extras.

The writer has been studying and commenting on customer relations for many years. The Saga product is one that stands out as a near perfect match between a particular customer base and the product offered. Sidney De Haan's ideas may have produced amusement in the early 1950s but they have proved to be a sound way forward for the company he founded.

## TIME LINE: SAGA

» **1951**: First Saga vacations offered as off-season breaks for 60+ age group.
» **1959**: No passport day trips by air to France from Lydd in Kent (UK).
» **1960**: Resort established in the Algarve (Portugal).
» **1966**: *Saga Club* established.
» **1970**: Vacations extended to Spain, Romania and Yugoslavia.
» **1979**: US office opened.
» **1984**: Saga Magazine launched. Sidney de Haan retires to be succeeded by his son Roger.
» **1985**: Saga awarded Queen's Award for Export Achievement.
» **1987**: Saga Services established to provide insurance, etc.
» **1988**: Second Queen's Award for Export Achievement awarded.
» **1995**: Qualifying age lowered from 60 to 50.
» **1996**: *Saga Rose* purchased.
» **2000**: PrimeTime digital radio launched.
» **2001**: Saga announces the charter of *Saga Pearl* from 2003.

### KEY INSIGHTS

» Niche markets can be entered successfully provided that the needs and wants of the customer base are understood.
» Know the customer and understand what it is they want.
» In the case of Saga the customer base is comfortable with paying up front rather than paying a lower initial price and then having extras added.
» Saga prices include items that many companies add on as extras.
» Customers can book everything direct without having to leave the comfort of their homes.
» Never underestimate the customer – the 50+ vacationer will go into the Arctic Circle (or anywhere else) provided that there is the proper back up facilities – in this case Saga Rose.

## CHOWKING FOOD CORPORATION

When the Chowking Food Corporation gained entrance to the Philippines' highly competitive fast food industry in 1985 it was at a time when the Philippines market was dominated by western-style burger outlets. US style fast food outlets have spread throughout the world with McDonalds, Burger King, and Kentucky Fried Chicken being household names to a global population of youngsters. The food served in these outlets, the vast majority of which are franchises, has often led to a decline in the popularity of local dishes especially in the youth market.

Chowking, founded by Robert Kuan, positioned itself in a niche where it could be a strong leader, by adopting the best features of two distinct restaurant styles. The first was that of the traditional Chinese restaurant with its menu of easy-to-prepare and reasonably-priced dishes. The second was the modern, western-style fast food outlet with its eye-catching façade, bright interiors and young staff dispensing friendly and speedy service. Kuan's concept was to merge the two styles into his unique concept: the Oriental quick-service restaurant. With a focus on superior product value and a high degree of customer care, Chowking has stood the test of shifting tastes, changing lifestyles and a volatile market to develop its own set of loyal customers that keeps growing year in and year out.

In 1989, in an aggressive bid to expand its client base and capture a bigger share of the market, the company initiated its franchising operations and marked its entry into the provincial market. By undertaking to franchise the operation Chowking followed the path taken by the most successful fast food companies. These twin moves enabled the company to pursue an ambitious expansion program that has made Chowking the largest Oriental quick-service chain in the Philippines, enjoying high visibility in all the major cities and towns in the country's main island groups of Luzon, Visayas, and Mindanao.

In 1995, based on its success in the Philippines domestic market, the company took the bold decision of venturing into the global market with the opening of a Chowking store in California. Currently Chowking outlets are operating in the US West Coast under a licensing agreement with a Filipino expatriate family. A similar agreement has been made with a Dubai national for the operation of Chowking stores in the Middle East. Many Filipinos work in the Middle East and thus there is a ready market for a product from their homeland.

Chowking is as aware as any franchiser of the importance of ensuring a uniform standard of product and customer care across the franchises.

A customer should not know whether an outlet is a franchise or not and should receive the same standard of service whether the outlet is in Manila, California, or Dubai.

The start of the twenty-first century brought a major new development. On 1 January 2000 Chowking became a wholly owned subsidiary of Jollibee Foods Corporation, the largest, most respected restaurant chain in the Philippines. The change of ownership gave rise to renovations and improvements, beginning with a fresh corporate image and a brand-new retail identity.

This identity manifests itself in almost all the physical aspects of the store – the logo, façade, layout, décor, counter, menu board, furniture, equipment and even the staff uniforms. Launched in June 2000, the new corporate look was introduced into all new outlets at their opening, while older outlets were renovated to conform to the new image. All these changes are complemented by front-end and back-end systems designed to ensure cost-efficiency, speed up service and increase customer satisfaction. Kuan is well aware that in the fast food business one does not have to win just the hearts and minds of the customers but their stomachs as well.

Hand in hand with the new physical features is the renewed pursuit of high standards in food, service, and cleanliness, the three most important aspects of the restaurant business. The company's mission is as fundamental as it is simple: "To serve consistently delicious and hot food in five minutes, amid sanitary and clean-smelling surroundings." This is precisely what the customer using a fast food outlet requires.

The strategic alliance between Chowking and Jollibee has proven mutually beneficial, bolstering their individual positions in the Philippine market – Jollibee as the undisputed market leader in the fast food industry; Chowking as the number one oriental quick-service restaurant chain. Jollibee lends its experience and prestige as the Philippines' dominant player in the fast food industry, while Chowking contributes significantly to the annual sales of the Jollibee group. Both companies are optimizing the advantages of the merger with synergies aimed at cutting costs and improving efficiency in their stores.

Kuan studied his customers carefully. In 1992 he was convinced that the large noodle meal often consumed in Asia as the main meal of the day could be promoted as an afternoon snack and that with the smaller quantities required for a snack the price could be lowered. That Kuan's careful study of his customers' eating habits had been worthwhile was evidenced by the fact that in the month of the introduction of the noodle snack, noodle sales increased by 40 percent and by as much as 50 percent in the following months. He also discovered that the rise in noodle sales produced a similar rise in dim sum (the assorted small items of savory food served as a light oriental meal) as customers could afford both the noodles and a dim sum order on the side.

Analyzing the customer base in 1994 Kuan noted that it was a bipolar base consisting of both teenagers and middle to upper income adults. The company appeared to be perceived by many as either for teenagers or adults only, thus alienating children and families. As these constitute a huge market the decision was made in 1995 to promote Chowking as a children's food chain in addition to one for adults. McDonald's in the UK carried out a similar promotion in 2002 but the other way around – they presented the chain as one for older adults in addition to the youth market.

The final market segment, that of low-income adults, was targeted next with a campaign that stressed the affordability and value for money of Chowking products. That produced a 24 percent increase in sales in June to August 1995.

By 2000 the operation had grown to 162 outlets, four of which were in the US and three in Dubai.

The change of ownership gave rise to renovations and improvements, beginning with a fresh corporate image made concrete by a brand new retail identity. All these changes were complemented by front-end and back-end systems designed to ensure cost-efficiency, speed up service, and increase customer satisfaction.

## TIME LINE: CHOWKING

» **1985**: Chowking enters Philippines fast food market.
» **1987**: First franchises granted.
» **1992**: Noodle snack introduced.
» **1995**: US and Dubai markets entered. Targeted campaigns at children, families and lower income earners.
» **2000**: Merger with Jollibee. 162 outlets in operation – 155 in the Philippines, 4 in the US, and 3 in Dubai.

## KEY INSIGHTS

» Studying the customer base can indicate future areas for expansion.

» Competitive advantage can be gained by combining different styles.

» Product and customer care standards need to be equal across all outlets whether they are franchised or not.

» Movement into markets with a ready customer base (such as Dubai with its large Filipino population) is a sensible form of expansion.

» No customer group should be ignored: targeting the low income market provided Chowking with a 24 percent increase in sales.

# Customer Relationships Key Concepts and Thinkers

This chapter consists of:

» a glossary for customer relations; and
» key thinkers in the field of customer relations.

The following is a glossary of customer relations.

**A-loyalty** – behavior displayed by satisfied customers who show no loyalty to any particular brand or supplier (see also mercenary).

**Added value** – the value added to a product or service along the customer chain. Added value represents the difference between the total cost of a product or service and what the customer is prepared to pay.

**Anti-loyalty** – behavior shown by some previously highly satisfied customers who feel that they have been let down so badly that they try to take revenge on the offending organization (see also terrorist).

**Apostles** – customers who are highly delighted with a supplier and/or brand over a period of time (see also supra–loyalty).

**Brand loyalty** – loyalty to a particular brand but not necessarily to a particular supplier/retailer.

**Core product** – the part of a product designed to meet the customer's main need requirements (see also supplementary product).

**Customer** – somebody for whom you satisfy a need.

**Customer chain** – the connection between the various internal and external customers of a product/service finishing with the end user.

**Customer driven** – an organizational approach in which the needs and wants of the customer drive developments, with the customer at the center of the organization.

**Customer orientation** – a philosophy in which the customer is an integral part of the organization's processes.

**De-loyalty** – behavior shown by a previously loyal customer who becomes dissatisfied and makes a deliberate choice to switch to another supplier or brand (see also defector).

**Defector** – a customer who makes a deliberate choice to switch to another supplier or brand (see also de-loyalty).

**E-commerce** – the use of the Internet to undertake commercial transactions.

**End user** – the final customer for a product/service.

**External customers** – those members of the customer chain who are outside the supplying organization.

**Grudge purchase** – the purchase of a product/service that the customer needs but does not either want or want to pay for, e.g. dentistry, prisons etc.

**Hostage** – a customer behavior typology representing a customer who appears loyal to a supplier or a product but in fact has no choice as the organization/product is operating in a monopoly (see also supra-loyalty).

**Internal customers** – those members of the customer chain who are inside the organization or its suppliers.

**Lifetime value** – the cumulative value or potential value of a customer's relationship with an organization over time.

**Loss leader** – something that is sold at below its value to elicit further business.

**Mail order** – a means of obtaining goods by ordering them from a catalogue for delivery by mail or courier service.

**Marketing orientation** – a philosophy based on the concept that the more that an organization knows about its customers and their requirements, the less effort will be needed in the sale's process.

**Mercenary** – satisfied customers who show no loyalty to any particular brand or supplier (see also a-loyalty).

**Monopoly** – a situation where there is only one supplier for a product or service thus giving the customer no choice at all.

**Needs** – products/services that a customer actually needs as opposed to wants (see also wants). Needs are often basic.

**Organizational body language** – the actual message that an organization puts out by way of ambience, facilities, signs etc. that provide a true gauge of its attitude to its customers.

**Product led** – an organizational approach in which the organization develops products and services with little actual market research and then "sells" the results to the customer base.

**Product orientation** – a philosophy that encompasses a belief that if products are of high enough quality and at a reasonable price, then sufficient customers will buy them.

**Pseudo-loyalty** – apparent loyalty that is caused by the customer having no alternatives (see hostage).

**Repeat business** – subsequent sales to the customer. Repeat business is a key performance indicator as it provides a measure of the relationship between the customer and the organization.

**Selling orientation** – a philosophy that recognizes that consumers may be reluctant to buy and need to be "sold" the product or service.

**Supplementary products** – extras to the core product.

**Supplier loyalty** – loyalty to a particular supplier/retailer. May be combined with brand loyalty.

**Supra-loyalty** – loyalty displayed by customers who are highly delighted with a supplier and/or brand over a period of time (see also apostles).

**Terrorist** – a type of previously highly satisfied customers who feel that they have been let down so badly that they try to take revenge on the offending organization (see also anti-loyalty).

**Wants** – products/services that the customer wants. These are often needs + supplementary products/services.

## KEY THINKERS

### David Clutterbuck

David Clutterbuck is one of Britain's most prominent management authors, with more than two dozen books on the subject including four major texts on customer relations. These are: *The Winning Streak* and *The Winning Streak Mark II*, both written with Walter Goldsmith, the former managing director of Black & Decker in the UK, *Inspired Customer Service* written with Graham Clark (from Cranfield University) and Colin Armistead (also from Cranfield University), and *Making Customers Count* with Susan Kernaghan.

Clutterbuck has been keen to stress that customer relations need to be implemented within a strategy that puts the customer at the center of an organization's activities. As he and his colleagues have pointed out, customer relations are not just for those in the front line but are an important part of the role of senior management.

Clutterbuck uses case studies from successful companies such as Reuters and Boots to illustrate the need for an holistic approach to customer relations.

### Relevant publications

*The Winning Streak* (with Goldsmith, W.), 1983.
*Making Customers Count* (with Kernaghan, S.), 1992.
*Inspired Customer Service* (with Clark, G. & Armistead, C.), 1993.
*The Winning Streak Mark II*, 1997.

## Bradley T. Gale

In *Managing Customer Value: Creating Quality & Service That Customers Can See*, Gale outlines the evolution of corporate America's efforts to measure customer values and customer retention. He provides case histories from Milliken, AT&T, United Van Lines, and Gillette, detailing the importance of customer satisfaction research in weighing such concepts as "market perceived quality" and "customer value analysis."

As a pragmatist Gale insists that customer research can be thrown out the window unless it is used to make businesses better. He is a former overseer of the Malcolm Baldrige National Quality Award.

### Relevant publications

*Managing Customer Value: Creating Quality & Service That Customers Can See* (with Chapman Wood, R.), 1994.

## Seth Godin

In *Permission Marketing* Godin argues that businesses can no longer rely solely on traditional forms of "interruption advertising" in magazines, mailings, or radio and television commercials. He states that today's consumers are bombarded by marketing messages almost everywhere they go. Given the huge amounts of advertising, if an organization wishes to grab someone's undivided attention, it first needs to get his or her permission with some kind of bait – a free sample, a big discount, a contest, an 0800 number, or even just an opinion survey.

Once a customer volunteers his or her time, the organization has taken the first step towards establishing a long-term relationship and making a sale. By talking only to volunteers, permission marketing guarantees that consumers pay more attention to the marketing message he writes. Godin believes that with permission marketing the customers and marketers enter into a symbiotic exchange where both gain.

Godin created Internet marketer Yoyodyne and sold it in 1998 to Yahoo, of which he is a vice president. Godin has analyzed the strategies of several companies that practice permission marketing successfully, including amazon.com (see Chapter 4 of this material), American Airlines, Bell Atlantic, and American Express. He believes that permission marketing is best suited to the Internet because the medium eliminates costs such as envelopes, printing, and stamps.

Godin has also written a large number of texts on other areas of business including the "If you are clueless about . . ." series.

### Relevant publications

*E-Marketing*, 1995.
*Permission Marketing*, 1999.

## George Green

George Green was a manager at British Rail from 1973 to 1986, much of the time in operations management. Since then he has run his own training consultancy, specializing in people and operations management. He has worked extensively with major organizations such as British Airways (throughout the world) and the Civil Aviation Authority.

In 1997 he worked with the writer of this material in the production of *In Charge of Customer Satisfaction* where they put forward the concept of "organizational body language" after research into the dissonance between the customer relations messages put out by organizations and the actual experience of the customer. Together George Green and the present writer produced their 10 Golden Rules for Customer Care.

1 It costs far more to gain a new customer than it does to retain an existing one.
2 Unless you recover the situation quickly, a lost customer will be lost for ever.
3 Dissatisfied customers have far more friends than satisfied ones.
4 The customer isn't always right, but how you tell them that they're wrong can make all the difference and ultimately they do pay your wages.
5 Welcome complaints – they allow for recovery.
6 In a free market economy never forget that the customer has a choice.
7 Treat internal customers as you would external ones.
8 You must listen to the customer to find out what they want.

9  If you don't believe, how can you expect the customer to?
10  If you don't look after your customers, somebody else will.

The point about using complaints to recover a situation and to enhance the customer relationship is one that is also stressed by Ros Jay (see later in this section).

## Relevant publications

*In Charge of Customer Satisfaction* (with Cartwright, R.), 1997.
*Operations and Technology*, 2002.
*Training & Development*, 2002.
*Developing Teams*, 2002.

## Ros Jay

Ros Jay is a marketing and communications specialist and author of *Smart Things to Know about Customers* in addition to a number of best selling texts on management, marketing and time management.

In *Smart Things to Know about Customers* Jay presents highly practical strategies that can be employed to carry through the concept of the customer at the center of the organization. Jay confronts the problem that all organizations experience – how to delight the customer when each and every customer wants something different?

By considering the customer service vision, how to become close to the customer and manage the relationship, using complaints as a positive means of gaining new business, using e-commerce and relationship marketing, Jay demonstrates how customer loyalty can be built up.

Jay has also written general management texts such as *Winning Minds – The Ultimate Book of Business Leadership* that also have implications for customer relations as the customer–supplier philosophy is an important component of the role of senior managers.

## Relevant texts

*The Seven Deadly Sins of Communicating*, 1998.
*Smart Things to Know about Customers*, 2000.
*Winning Minds – the Ultimate Book of Business Leadership*, 2001.

## Jones & Sasser

Frequent contributors to the Harvard Business Review, Jones and Sasser have an international reputation especially in the study of loyalty. Jones is the President of Elm Square Technologies and Sasser is the UPS Professor of Service Management at Harvard Business School.

They developed the apostle, loyalist, mercenary, defector, hostage, and terrorist typology considered in Chapter 6 of this material. One of their most important contributions to the field of customer relations has been to describe how mere satisfaction is no longer enough to guarantee loyalty.

### Relevant texts

*Customer Loyalty: Keeping Customers*, 1990.
*Putting the Service Profit Chain to Work* (with Heskett, J.L., Loveman, G.W. & and Schlesinger, L.A.), 1994.
*Why Satisfied Customers Defect*, 1995.

## Tom Peters

Whilst there are those who feel that it might be passé to include Tom Peters in this section, the contribution that both Peters and his colleague Bob Waterman have made to customer relations is very important.

*In Search of Excellence* in 1982 contained "closeness to the customer" as an attribute of the excellent companies Peters and Waterman were examining. They were amongst the first to show how the world of business had changed from a product orientation to a customer orientation as detailed in Chapter 3 of this material.

Since then Tom Peters has become one of the best known names in the fields of management, change and quality. His message has been delivered on a global basis and has reached a huge audience, initially of senior but more recently including junior staff.

Three quotes express the importance Tom Peters has had on modern organizational thinking:

> "In no small part, what American corporations have become is what Peters has encouraged them to be."
>
> *The New Yorker*

"Peters is . . . the father of the post-modern corporation."

*Los Angeles Times*

"We live in a Tom Peters world."

*Fortune Magazine*

Tom Peters describes himself as a prince of disorder, champion of bold failures, maestro of zest, professional loudmouth, corporate cheerleader, and a lover of markets, *Fortune Magazine* has also referred to him as the Ur-guru (guru of gurus) of management and compares him to Ralph Waldo Emerson, Henry David Thoreau, and Walt Whitman. *The Economist* has titled him as the Uber-guru (literally over-guru). His unconventional views led *Business Week* to describe him as business' best friend and worst nightmare. Best friend because of the challenges he throws out which if taken up can lead to success, and worst nightmare because his ideas have challenged conventional thinking – always an uncomfortable thing to do.

Tom followed up on the success of *In Search of Excellence* (1982, with Robert Waterman) with three more best-selling hardback books – *A Passion for Excellence* (1985, with Nancy Austin), *Thriving on Chaos* (1987), and *Liberation Management* (1992, acclaimed as the management book of the decade) – books that linked, as part of their theme, the need to be close to the customer.

Tom Peters also presents about 100 major seminars globally each year. Organizations pay considerable sums for their staff to attend these seminars. He has also authored hundreds of articles for various newspapers and popular and academic journals, including *Business Week*, *The Economist*, the *Financial Times*, *The Wall Street Journal*, *The New York Times, Inc.*, *Fast Company*, *The Washington Monthly*, *California Management Review*, *The Academy of Management Review*, *Forbes*, and *The Harvard Business Review*.

## Relevant publications

*In Search of Excellence* (with Waterman, R.), 1982.
*A Passion For Excellence* (with Austin, N.), 1985.
*Thriving on Chaos*, 1987.
*Liberation Management*, 1992.

## Michael Porter

A renowned professor at Harvard Business School, Porter has been the world authority on competition and competitive strategies since the 1980s. His writing has informed both those in industry and academia on the nature of competition and the forces that drive the process. It was Porter who introduced the famous "5 Forces" model: the bargaining power of the supplier, the bargaining power of the customer, competition between existing players, the threat of new entrants, and the treat of substitution, that has been used by many to explain how the competitive process has worked in particular industries.

The relative bargaining power of the customer has been increasing in recent years especially as e-commerce has given customers ever-increasing choices. Whilst much of Porter's work was written prior to the use of the Internet for commerce it is still as relevant today as it was when the traditional means of doing business were all that were available.

In *The Competitive Advantage of Nations* he turned his ideas and his attention to the global stage. In this text he identified the fundamental determinants of national competitive advantage in an industry and how they work together to give international advantage. The findings had implications for firms and governments and set the agenda for discussions of global competition. The most relevant of his books for this material are listed below:

### Relevant publications

*Competitive Advantage*, 1980.
*Cases in Competitive Strategy*, 1982.
*Competitive Strategy*, 1985.
*On Competition*, 1998.
*The Competitive Advantage of Nations*, 1998, new revised edition.

## Patricia Seybold

Patricia Seybold's influential book *Customers.com* draws on case studies of companies and organizations as diverse as Boeing, Babson College, National Semiconductor, Hertz, PhotoDisc, and Wells Fargo. Seybold identifies what makes e-commerce work successfully. She argues that any e-commerce initiative has to begin with the customer. Seybold points out that in the world of Internet commerce, knowing who the customers are and making sure that the organization has the products and services they want becomes even more imperative than it is in traditional business relationships. Once customers can go anywhere to get what they want, the organizations seeking their business need to know exactly what the customers are looking for.

*Customers.com* contains 16 case studies of organizations that have successfully embraced e-business and e-commerce. Each is well researched, and includes an executive summary with details of what each organization did right.

Seybold is the founder and CEO of the Boston-based Patricia Seybold Group that deals with strategic insight, technology guidance, and e-business best practices. Seybold has more than 20 years of computer industry consulting experience.

In all her writing Seybold takes a practical approach to managing customer relations in a virtual, e-commerce environment. In her latest book, *The Customer Revolution*, she establishes how to measure and monitor what matters most to a company's fundamental source of value, its customers. Not surprisingly given the nature of her subject much of Seybold's work is available in e-book format.

*Relevant publications*

*Customers.com*, 1998.
*Dotcom Divas*, (with Carlassare, E.), 2001.
*The Customer Revolution*, 2001.

## George S. Yip

A teacher of business strategy and international marketing at UCLA and a former faculty member at Harvard Business School, Yip has written a useful guide on the processes involved in reaching the global marketplace with its global consumers in his book *Total Global Strategy*. Very much concerned with the gaining of competitive advantage, Yip provides clear practical advice on global marketing, product design, competition, and the structure of a global organization. His comments on global customers are made from the viewpoint of the purchasing patterns of large corporate customers. He points out that the bargaining power of such customers (see the entry on Michael Porter earlier in this section) is massive and can act as a driving force within the particular market.

Well qualified to comment on global organizations as he is Asian by birth, Yip lives in the US and has EU citizenship, Yip has also written on developing strategies for Central and Eastern European expansion and on expanding into Asian markets.

## Relevant book

*Total Global Strategy*, 1992.

## Richard C. Whiteley

Vice-chair and co-founder of the Forum Corporation, Whiteley provides detailed information and strategies in order to achieve customer centered growth.

He points out, quite rightly, that customer centered growth is the most lasting type of growth and that organizations that are customer centered will find that they are more able to cope with changing customer demands due to the intelligence they receive by being close to the customer.

## Relevant publications

*The Customer Driven Company*, 1991.
*Customer Centered Growth* (with Hessan, D.), 1996.

# Resources on Customer Relationships

This chapter is concerned with where to find resources on the development and maintaining of customer relationships.

This chapter focuses on book, journal and Website resources, but please note that the dates of books in this chapter may differ from those shown previously. The dates here are editions that have been revised from the date of first publication as shown in the chapter material.

Alsop, R. (1989) "Brand loyalty is rarely blind loyalty", *Wall St Journal*, 19 Oct 1989, pb1 Bradley, G.T.

Cartwright, R. (2000), *Mastering Customer Relations*, Macmillan-Palgrave, Basingstoke.

Cartwright, R. (2002), *Going Global*, Capstone, Oxford.

Cartwright, R. & Green, G. (1997), *In Charge of Customer Satisfaction*, Blackwell, Oxford.

Celsi, T. (1991), *Ralph Nader - The Consumer Revolution*, Millbrook, Brookfield (CT).

Clutterbuck, D. Clark, G. & Armistead, C. (1993), *Inspired Customer Service*, Kogan Page, London.

Clutterbuck, D. & Goldsmith, W. (1983), *The Winning Streak*, Orion, London.

Clutterbuck, D. & Goldsmith, W. (1997), *The Winning Streak Mark II*, Orion, London.

Clutterbuck, D. & Kernaghan, S. (1992), *Making Customers Count*, Mercury, London.

Davie, M. (1986), *Titanic - The Full Story of a Tragedy*, Bodley Head, London.

Davies, C. (1997), *Divided by a Common Language*, Mayflower Press, Sarasota (FL).

Gale, B.T. & Wood, R.C. (1994), *Managing Customer Value: Creating Quality & Service That Customers Can See*, Free Press, New York.

Godin, S. (1995), *E-marketing*, Berkeley, San Francisco.

Godin, S. (1999), *Permission Marketing*, Simon & Schuster, New York.

Green, G. (2002), *Operations and Technology*, Capstone, Oxford.

Green, G. (2002), *Training & Development*, Capstone, Oxford.

Green, G. (2002), *Developing Teams*, Capstone, Oxford.

Harris, P.R. & Moran, R.T. (2000), *Managing Cultural Differences*, Gulf Publishing Co., Houston.

Harvey, D. (2002), *Customers - The Hidden Threat to Your Business*, Capstone, Oxford.

Herzberg, F. (1962), *Work and the Nature of Man*, World Publishing, New York.

Honey, P. (1990), *Face to Face Skills*, Gower, London.

Jay, R. (1998), *The Seven Deadly Sins of Communicating*, International Thomson Business Press, London.

Jay, R. (2000), *Smart Things to Know about Customers*, Capstone, Oxford.

Jay, R. (2001), *Winning Minds - the Ultimate Book of Business Leadership*, Capstone, Oxford.

Jones, T.O. & Sasser, W.E. Jnr (1990), *Customer Loyalty: Keeping Customers*, Harvard Business School Press, Cambridge (MA).

Jones, T.O., Sasser, W.E. Jnr, Heskett, J.L., Loveman, G.W. & Schlesinger, L.A. (1994), "Putting the service profit chain to work", *Harvard Business Review*, March–April 1994, pp. 164–174, *Harvard Business Review*, Cambridge (MA).

Jones, T.O. & Sasser, W.E. Jnr (1995), "Why satisfied customers defect", *Harvard Business Review*, Nov–Dec 1995 pp 88-99, *Harvard Business Review*, Cambridge (MA).

Lewis, R.D. (2000), *When Cultures Collide*, Nicholas Brealey, London.

Maslow, A. (1970), *Motivation and Personality*, Harper & Row, New York.

Nader, R. (1965), *Unsafe at Any Speed*, Grossman, New York.

Peters, T. & Waterman, R. (1982), *In Search of Excellence*, Harper & Row, New York.

Peters, T. & Austin, N. (1994), *A Passion For Excellence*, HarperCollins, New York.

Peters, T. (1992), *Liberation Management*, Alfred A. Knopf, New York.

Peters, T. (1989), *Thriving on Chaos*, New York, HarperCollins.

Porter, M. (1980), *Competitive Advantage*, Free Press, New York.

Porter, M. (1985), *Competitive Strategy*, Free Press, New York.

Porter, M. (1992), *Cases in Competitive Strategy*, Free Press, New York.

Porter, M. (1998), *On Competition*, Harvard Business School Press, Cambridge (MA).

Porter, M. (1998), *The Competitive Advantage of Nations*, Macmillan, Basingstoke.

Sabbach, K. (1995), *21st Century Jet – the Making of the Boeing* 777, Macmillan, Basingstoke.

Seybold, P.B. (1998), *Customers.com*, Random House, New York.

Seybold, P.B. & Carlassare E, (2001), *Dotcom Divas*, McGraw Hill, New York.

Seybold, P.B & Smith, C. (ed), (2001), *The Customer Revolution*, Random House, New York.

Stauffer, D. (2000), *Business the AOL Way*, Capstone, Oxford.

Trompenaars, F. (1993), *Riding the Waves of Culture*, Economist Books, London.

Whiteley, R.C. (1991), *The Customer Driven Company*, Random House, New York.

Whiteley, R.C. & Hessan, D. (1997), *Customer-Centered Growth*, Addison Wesley, New York.

Wind, J. (1982), *Product, Policy and Concepts, Methods and Strategy*, Addison-Wesley, New York.

Yip, G.S. (1992), *Total Global Strategy*, Prentice Hall, Eaglewood Cliffs (NJ).

For information about Boeing and the 777:

Sabbach, K. (1995), *21st Century Jet – the Making of the Boeing* 777, Macmillan, Basingstoke.

For information about Amazon:

Saunders, R. (2001), *Business the Amazon Way*, Capstone, Oxford.

Spector, R. (2000), *Amazon.com*, Random House, London.

## JOURNALS ETC.

### The Customer Care Institute (Atlanta)

The Customer Care Institute (CCI) is a global resource organization serving customer care professionals. It focuses on customer care issues found in the consumer affairs, customer service, teleservices and help desk professions. The institute provides:

» research;
» advisory services; and

» training and networking opportunities for customer care professionals.

The Institute conducts studies, publishes white papers, booklets and newsletters, organizes forums, workshops and conferences, and offers other programs and services that will enhance the delivery of customer care.
www.customercare.com

### Customer Interface Magazine

This is the ICCM journal of management and technology strategies for customer contact professionals.

Published monthly in the US, *Customer Interface* is a business management resource for senior and mid-level decision-makers who are responsible for call centers, customer contact and CRM initiatives.

The magazine has been published for more than 15 years and is the "must read" monthly publication for call center managers, supervisors, and corporate executives.
www.c-interface.com

### Customer Services

The magazine of the UK Institute of Customer Service, containing information about training and development linked to the provision of customer service.
www.instcustserve.com

### Forbes

Forbes is a leading resources provider for the world's business and investment leaders, providing commentary, analysis, relevant tools, and real-time reporting.

The weekly *Forbes* magazine is also available online and whilst mainly designed for the US audience it is read on a global basis. *Forbes* often carries articles and commentaries that are relevant to customer relations.

Other linked products from Forbes include *Forbes Global* which covers the rise of capitalism around the world for international business leaders. It contains sections on companies and industry, capital markets and investing, entrepreneurs, technology, and Forbes global life.

There are also Forbes newsletters which include: *Forbes Aggressive Growth Investor*, recommending the fifty best growth and momentum stocks to own now as determined by a proprietary multi-dimensional computer analysis of over 3000 stocks; *Gilder Technology Report*, covering the smartest, most profitable way to invest in technology–the *Gilder Technology Report* will show you how to buy tomorrow's biggest technology winners today when their shares are cheap and you can potentially multiply your wealth 10 to 100 times; *Special Situation Survey* has monthly stock recommendations, hold or sell advice on each recommendation and special investment reports; *New Economy Watch* is a newsletter that looks at Internet based companies.
www.forbes.com

## Harvard Business Review

A leading business and management resource. Read worldwide and featuring contributions by the leading names in business and management. Jones and Sasser (see Chapters 6 and 8 of this material) have been frequent contributors. Published 10 times per annum and available by subscription.
www.hbsp.harvard.edu/products/hbr

## Journal of Consumer Culture

A printed journal published by Sage Publications that is also available online. The journal aims to publish groundbreaking debates and articles that focus on consumption and consumer culture including:

» Consumerism
» Culture
» Globalization
» Consumers
» Customers
» Sociology of consumption
» Consumer societies

www.sagepub.co.uk/journals/details/j0349.html

## Journal of Consumer Satisfaction, Dissatisfaction and Complaining Behavior

An annual publication from the Washington State University in Vancouver, the journal carries academic articles on issues related to customer behavior.
www.vancouver.wsu/edu/csdcb

## Journal of Retailing and Consumer Services

The journal is an international and interdisciplinary forum for research and debate in the rapidly developing – and converging – fields of retailing and services studies. Published quarterly, it focuses particularly on consumer behavior and on policy and managerial decisions, encouraging contributions both from practitioners in the forefront of new developments in retailing and services, and from academics across a wide range of relevant disciplines.

Designed for a wide audience from academics and students in relevant disciplines including business and management, marketing, urban planning, geography, economics, leisure science, travel and tourism, to senior managers in industry, commerce, and public services, and consultants in such areas as economic and business forecasting, corporate planning, and strategic management, the journal covers:

» the distribution and selling of goods;
» the retailing of professional services such as health and law;
» the retailing of consumer services such as transportation, tourism, leisure, and personal financial services; and
» issues of education and training for employers and course providers.

www.elsevier.nl/locatel/retconser

## Management Today

From the Institute of Management in the UK, monthly to members or by subscription. Often contains useful articles on issues concerned with training and especially with management development. The institute also provides management development programs in association with approved providers.
www.inst-man.org.uk

## *The Quarterly Journal of Electronic Commerce*

This is a scholarly international journal focused on the emerging field of electronic commerce. The journal addresses e-commerce with a broad, interdisciplinary approach. It establishes the field's intellectual foundation with state-of-the-art research from business, computer science, engineering, law, psychology, and sociology. One of the Journal's primary objectives is to facilitate the growth of internet-based e-commerce. This, together with the cross-disciplinary approach, distinguishes the journal from more narrowly focused journals in the field. Topics covered include:

» electronic marketing;
» consumer marketing;
» interactive advertising;
» trading and marketing systems technologies;
» net based payment and electronic cash;
» internet-enabled smart card applications;
» internet gambling;
» internet commercial law;
» regulation and taxation;
» security and internet;
» commercial crime;
» open electronic publishing technologies; and
» public confidence and participant trust.

www.qjec.org

## WEBSITES

www.amazon.com – the main Amazon.com Website.
www.amazon.co.uk – the Amazon UK Website.
www.boeing.com – Boeing's Website.
www.chowking.com – the Chowking Website
www.jessops.com – Jessops Website (see Chapter 10)
www.kalmbach.com – the Kalmbach Publications Website.
www.saga.co.uk – the Saga Website.

# Ten Steps to Effective Customer Relations

» Never neglect existing customers in order to gain new ones.
» Recover problem situations as promptly as possible.
» Always aim for a win/win situation.
» The customer isn't always right, but how you tell them that they're wrong can make all the difference.
» Delight rather than mere satisfaction.
» Remember that in a free market economy the customer has a choice.
» Treat internal customers as you would external ones.
» Listen to the customer to find out what they want.
» Be positive about your products and services.
» Walk the talk – use OBL to discover what impression you give out to your customers.

## 1. NEVER NEGLECT EXISTING CUSTOMERS IN ORDER TO GAIN NEW ONES

Whilst the gaining of new customers may be glamorous there is little point to it if existing customers perceive that they are no longer as important to the organization and thus defect to a competitor.

It costs at least two and a half times as much to gain a new customer as to retain an existing one. That cost is made up of marketing and advertising costs plus the costs of discounts and loss leaders used to attract new customers. For every existing customer who is lost there is a need to gain not one replacement but two and a half new customers.

Whilst this may seem common sense there are many instances on record of organizations that have put all of their effort into new customers and have ended up in major financial difficulty due to a leaking away of their original customer base. Those existing customers do not disappear; more often than not they go to a competitor and the customer accumulator discussed in Chapter 6 comes into effect.

## 2. RECOVER PROBLEM SITUATIONS AS PROMPTLY AS POSSIBLE

No organization, product or service will be perfect all of the time. At some point in the supplier–customer relationship there will be a problem or complaint. In many instances it is not the original complaint that gives rise to continuing customer dissatisfaction but rather the inability or slowness of the organization to rectify the situation.

If the organization is able to show by a highly responsive attitude that it values the customer the negative complaint can be transformed into a positive strengthening of customer loyalty. We tend to remember the last thing that happened and if that last thing was the organization pulling out all the stops to resolve a problem this is the lasting memory the customer will retain.

The longer an issue is allowed to fester the more aggrieved the customer will become until nothing that the organization can do will retain him or her.

Complaints can be a useful source of feedback. Customer feedback should always be encouraged. It is calculated that for every customer who voices a complaint there may be nine others who say nothing but are nevertheless dissatisfied and may be reluctant to use the organization, its products, or its services again.

Dissatisfied customers tend, paradoxically, to have more friends than satisfied ones – that is we are far more likely to tell our friends, family, and colleagues about things that have gone wrong with a supplier or product than we are to tell them how good something is.

## 3. ALWAYS AIM FOR A WIN/WIN SITUATION

The four outcomes to any transaction; win/win, lose/win, win/lose and lose/lose were introduced in Chapter 3. The customer should never lose. Customers who end up on the losing side in a transaction are very unlikely to use the supplier or the product again.

Whilst an organization may be willing to lose in the short term through the use of discounts and loss leaders it will not be able to sustain such a strategy for long.

Two ways that both the organization and the customer can win are:

» a loss by the organization after a problem in order to retain the loyalty of the customer; or
» a loyalty bonus that entails the organization making slightly less on each transaction but with this offset by increased sales to the customer. It is better to sell 100 products to a customer and make $5 on each sale than to sell 50 and make $7!

If the customer were always to win at the expense of the supplier losing then the supplier would go out of business and the choices for the customer would be reduced.

## 4. THE CUSTOMER ISN'T ALWAYS RIGHT, BUT HOW YOU TELL THEM THAT THEY'RE WRONG CAN MAKE ALL THE DIFFERENCE

Customers are often wrong. Customers may have unreasonable expectations and they may be rude. It remains a fact that without customers there would be no organization. Sales staff need to be able to tell a customer that he or she is wrong without either insulting them or being patronizing.

There is an anecdotal story of an auto salesperson who always used to keep a one twenty-fourth die cast model of a vehicle on his desk. Whenever a customer demanded more and more discounts the salesperson would bring the model out and tell them "I can let you have this at what you are offering." Apparently the humor was just what was needed and the person won a number of sales awards. This showed the customer that he or she was being unreasonable by using humor. Nevertheless one needs to be very careful about how humor is used.

Whatever you may think about your customers, at the end of the day it is the customer who pays your wages. Seeing customers in terms of your house, your automobile, your vacation, and your family's well-being may make them seem less of a nuisance.

At the end of the day however, everybody should have the right to decline custom from those who are rude or too demanding. Doing so however carries the risk that the rejected customer may have some unpleasant things to say about the organization.

## 5. DELIGHT RATHER THAN MERE SATISFACTION

As customers get more and more choice, merely giving satisfaction is less likely to engender loyalty. It is delight that strengthens loyalty. Organizations can only delight their customers if they become close to them and listen to what it is the customer wants not only from the core but also the supplementary product.

Delight need not cost. A level of service over and above that expected may cause delight. At the end of this chapter there is a short case study where a small electric bulb caused delight to a customer and gained hundreds of dollars in extra business for an organization.

## 6. REMEMBER THAT IN A FREE MARKET ECONOMY THE CUSTOMER HAS A CHOICE

As markets become increasingly global no organization can afford to be complacent about the loyalty of its customers. Too many seemingly loyal customers have turned out to be hostages (see Chapter 6) and have defected to a competitor as soon as the opportunity presents itself.

Organizations need to keep in close contact with customers whenever the opportunity presents itself. The relationship between supplier and customer is strengthened after each successful interaction. The interaction does not need to be a sale. A telephone call to ask how the customer is finding a purchase will strengthen the relationship and provide an opportunity to rectify any problems.

## 7. TREAT INTERNAL CUSTOMERS AS YOU WOULD EXTERNAL ONES

The customer chain (Chapter 2) begins with internal customers and ends with external ones. If internal customers do not feel that there is a good relationship between them and the person supplying them or the customer they supply, quality tends to suffer.

Quality needs to be maintained all along the chain and thus the internal customer is just as important as the external one.

## 8. LISTEN TO THE CUSTOMER TO FIND OUT WHAT THEY WANT

The days of organizations deciding what to offer and then trying to sell it are fast disappearing. The only way to find out what the customer requires is to listen. The more information that comes direct from customers, the better the development and marketing strategies that the organization puts into place will be. If people talk and we don't listen they tend to go away. Customer relations works to the same principles–one of the fastest ways to lose a customer is to ignore them.

## 9. BE POSITIVE ABOUT YOUR PRODUCTS AND SERVICES

Those working for an organization must always show a positive image about the organization and its products to the customer. It is said that a major automobile plant had two parking lots. The one that could be seen from the road was for employees driving the company's products. Those with automobiles from other manufacturers had to park round the back. The company view was that if potential customers saw that the company's workers drove the products of competitors they might begin to wonder what was wrong with the company's product.

## 10 WALK THE TALK – USE OBL TO DISCOVER WHAT IMPRESSION YOU GIVE OUT TO YOUR CUSTOMERS

It is always worth approaching your place of work, not as an employee but as a customer. What messages are given out?

This can be a very fruitful exercise. In one case it showed that a direction sign was positioned wrongly. For six months nobody on the staff appeared to notice until an organizational body language audit was carried out.

Put yourself in the customer's shoes and then ask: am I welcome here?

## FINAL CASE

### Jessops

One of the trends that began towards the end of the twentieth century was the move from specialist retailers to more general operations in the areas of electronics, computing, and photography. Amateur photography has changed considerably since the days of the box Brownie. Today there is a bewildering choice of films, formats and cameras with digital photography growing at a considerable rate.

In the UK there is a long established national chain of photographic equipment retailers named Jessops.

The company is the United Kingdom's leading specialist retailer of photographic equipment and accessories. Operating from a network of over 200 stores nationwide, Jessops sells a comprehensive range of cameras, camcorders, digital photographic products, binoculars, and accessories in the country.

Jessops also offers a vast range of developing and printing services from traditional 35mm and APS processing to digital imaging services. Jessops has related activities that cater for the wholesale, commercial, professional, and the insurance markets.

The company was formed in the 1930s and over the years has built a strong reputation for the service it gives to both amateur and professional photographers. With its expanding store network the company is now extending its appeal to a wider clientele, whilst still retaining specialist status. Jessops has won numerous awards for customer service, including *Practical Photography* magazine's coveted Reader's Choice Award for "best photographic retailer" four years in a row.

Jessops is also a driving force in selling products using new technology. This is demonstrated by the phenomenal interest generated by digital cameras and camcorders. Jessops recognized very early on the importance that products such as these would have in the market and invested heavily in furnishing every store with full demonstration facilities and staff training. This has put Jessops in a unique position that allows it to offer industry-leading service and advice to customers on the very latest technology.

The commitment Jessops shows for customer service is only matched by the company's commitment to photography as a whole. Jessops prides itself on the fact that the majority of employees in its stores are keen photographers themselves. This means that customers can expect excellent service and great deals, plus expert advice on anything from a single use camera to a complete studio set-up.

The Jessops catalogue contains not only products but also advice and tips. There is a comprehensive Web site and the company even organizes training programs for customers.

A Jessops customer purchased a considerable amount of equipment worth around $600 from the nearest local store, albeit one that was a 50-mile round trip from home. After about six weeks the only problem was a blown bulb in a hand-held slide viewer. The bulb blew just days before the customer was to make an important slide presentation to a foreign audience.

One quick telephone call, a wait of 24 hours and a package had arrived in the mail with the bulb carefully secured in a plastic film can. There was no charge and the postage cost more than the bulb. A loss to Jessops?

Four weeks later the customer purchased additional equipment from the store worth another $400. The few cents cost of the bulb and postage provided hundreds of dollars worth of business. Many large chain stores might not have bothered with something so trivial but Jessops did and now have a loyal customer.

## KEY LEARNING POINTS

1 Never neglect existing customers in order to gain new ones.
2 Recover problem situations as promptly as possible.
3 Always aim for a win/win situation.
4 The customer isn't always right, but how you tell them that they're wrong can make all the difference.
5 Delight rather than merely satisfy.
6 Remember that in a free market economy the customer has a choice.
7 Treat internal customers as you would external ones.
8 Listen to the customer to find out what they want.
9 Be positive about your products and services.
10 Walk the talk – use OBL to discover what impression you give out to your customers.

# Frequently Asked Questions (FAQs)

### Q1: Surely the customer isn't always right are they?

A: No they are not. They are often wrong and have unrealistic expectations. Nevertheless they are the people who bring money into the organization. The skill is to point out their errors without being insulting or patronizing.

You can read more about this in Chapter 1.

### Q2: What is the lifetime value of the customer?

A: The sales that have already been made to that customer plus the potential future sales if he or she remains a customer.

You can read more about this in Chapter 2.

### Q3: What is the difference between satisfying the customer and delighting him or her?

A: Satisfaction is the minimum that the customer should expect. In a competitive market the customer usually wants to be delighted. Needs are satisfied, wants are delighted.

You can read more about this in Chapters 2, 3 and 6.

## Q4: Can complaints be positive?

A: Yes – complaints provide an opportunity for the organization to rectify problems and to show the customer that he or she is valued. You can read more about this in Chapters 6 and 10.

## Q5: Why is repeat business so important?

A: Repeat business depends on the relationship that has built up since the initial sale and is thus a measure of the strength of that relationship. You can read more about this in Chapters 2, 3 and 6.

## Q6: What is the difference between an internal and an external customer?

A: In terms of how they should be treated, none! Internal customers are that part of the customer/value chain inside the organization. You can read more about this in Chapter 2.

## Q7: What is meant by a hostage?

A: This is a term introduced by Jones and Sasser to describe a seemingly loyal customer who is not actually loyal but just has no choice in the supplier/product used. The Internet has helped "free" many hostages. You can read more about this in Chapters 4, 5 and 6.

## Q8: What is the customer accumulator?

A: A mathematical formula demonstrating that if a customer is lost to a competitor the net loss and respective gain is two and not one. You can read more about this in Chapter 6.

## Q9: How can organizational body language (OBL) be used?

A: OBL can be used to consider the customer experience through the actual messages that the organization puts out rather than those it claims. You can read more about this in Chapters 6 and 10.

## Q10: Where are resources available to assist in understanding the customer relations aspects of sales?

A: A list of books, journals and Web addresses will be found in Chapter 9.

# Index

# EXPRESSEXEC –
# BUSINESS THINKING AT YOUR FINGERTIPS

ExpressExec is a 12-module resource with 10 titles in each module. Combined they form a complete resource of current business practice. Each title enables the reader to quickly understand the key concepts and models driving management thinking today.

## Innovation

01.01 *Innovation Express*
01.02 *Global Innovation*
01.03 *E-Innovation*
01.04 *Creativity*
01.05 *Technology Leaders*
01.06 *Intellectual Capital*
01.07 *The Innovative Individual*
01.08 *Taking Ideas to Market*
01.09 *Creating an Innovative Culture*
01.10 *Managing Intellectual Property*

## Enterprise

02.01 *Enterprise Express*
02.02 *Going Global*
02.03 *E-Business*
02.04 *Corporate Venturing*
02.05 *Angel Capital*
02.06 *Managing Growth*
02.07 *Exit Strategies*
02.08 *The Entrepreneurial Individual*
02.09 *Business Planning*
02.10 *Creating the Entrepreneurial Organization*

## Strategy

03.01 *Strategy Express*
03.02 *Global Strategy*
03.03 *E-Strategy*
03.04 *The Vision Thing*
03.05 *Strategies for Hypergrowth*
03.06 *Complexity and Paradox*
03.07 *The New Corporate Strategy*
03.08 *Balanced Scorecard*
03.09 *Competitive Intelligence*
03.10 *Future Proofing*

## Marketing

04.01 *Marketing Express*
04.02 *Global Marketing*
04.03 *E-Marketing*
04.04 *Customer Relationship Management*
04.05 *Reputation Management*
04.06 *Sales Promotion*
04.07 *Channel Management*
04.08 *Branding*
04.09 *Market Research*
04.10 *Sales Management*

## Finance

05.01 *Finance Express*
05.02 *Global Finance*
05.03 *E-Finance*
05.04 *Investment Appraisal*
05.05 *Understanding Accounts*
05.06 *Shareholder Value*
05.07 *Valuation*
05.08 *Strategic Cash Flow Management*
05.09 *Mergers and Acquisitions*
05.10 *Risk Management*

## Operations and Technology

06.01 *Operations and Technology Express*
06.02 *Operating Globally*
06.03 *E-Processes*
06.04 *Supply Chain Management*
06.05 *Crisis Management*
06.06 *Project Management*
06.07 *Managing Quality*
06.08 *Managing Technology*
06.09 *Measurement and Internal Audit*
06.10 *Making Partnerships Work*

Available from:
www.expressexec.com

Customer Service Department
John Wiley & Sons Ltd
Southern Cross Trading Estate
1 Oldlands Way, Bognor Regis
West Sussex, PO22 9SA
Tel:    +44(0)1243 843 294
Fax:   +44(0)1243 843 303
Email: cs-books@wiley.co.uk